SOCRATES, PLATO, AND GUYS LIKE ME

Eric E. Rofes

Socrates, Plato, & guys like Me

Confessions of a gay schoolteacher

like Me

Boston · Alyson Publications, Inc.

This is a paperback original from Alyson Publications, Inc.,
PO Box 2783, Boston, MA 02208.
Distributed in England by GMP Publishers,
PO Box 247, London, N15 6RW.

First edition, July 1985   5 4 3 2 1

ISBN 0 932870 67 8

The events described here are true, and many of them are a matter of
public record. However, to help protect the privacy of certain
individuals, some names and identifying characteristics, including the
name of the school, have been changed.

— Eric Rofes

For
Tom Hehir

ACKNOWLEDGEMENTS

Some of the names and identifying characteristics of people and places in this book have been changed to protect the privacy of particular individuals. The substance of the book, and the actual events described, occurred between September, 1976 and June, 1978.

I wish to thank Paul Stein, Richard Burns, Linda Brown and Sasha Alyson for reading the original manuscript and providing me with critical feedback.

—— 1 ——

I opened the closet door and confronted my wardrobe. What would be the appropriate fashion statement for this new teacher to make on the first day of school? Bluejeans and t-shirts were clearly unacceptable, although they made up the bulk of the clothing in my possession. I picked up a green pastel Lacoste shirt and held it up to my chest in front of the mirror. Too feminine, I thought, and clearly too gay. Anyway, I was supposed to be an authority figure for young children. My black leather jacket would connote power and authority, but perhaps would be a bit much for the first day of school.

I finally selected a sports coat and khaki slacks. Since I intended to mold my appearance into that of the wizened, experienced New England schoolmaster, I slicked back my hair, clipped my beard clean around the edges, and put on the tortoise--shell eyeglasses I'd worn through college. I selected a crimson tie — the tie that had seen me through countless sherry-hours at Harvard — and white oxford shirt. Looking in the mirror before sprinting out the front door, I hardly recognized myself. The man gazing back appeared mature, responsible, confident and straight. Who was that stranger in the mirror?

Arriving at school, I signed the register at the office and was greeted by the school secretary. "You're looking spiffy, Mr.

Rofes," she said in her ever-friendly voice. "I'm looking forward to seeing what you'll look like at three o'clock this afternoon. Good luck with all those kids and try to have a nice first day of school."

I grabbed the papers from my mailbox, gave a quick farewell smile, and walked briskly down the corridor leading to the classrooms. As I passed the door to the library, I saw Alice, the librarian, and stuck my head in to wish her a good morning.

"You look great, Eric," she said warmly, her round, smiling face radiating a sense of calm that was unusual for the first day of school. "But I'm afraid I almost didn't recognize you. I suppose a little sharp dressing is in order on the first day of school."

"Just wish me luck, Alice," I said. "I'm about to be eaten alive."

"I'm sure you'll have a wonderful day. Don't believe what those cynics in the office tell you about your kids. You've got a big class, and they're bright, energetic and a lot of fun. You'll have your hands full, for sure. If you can keep your sense of humor with them, you'll do just fine. Now hurry off, the doors will open in five minutes and you'll find yourself surrounded by sixth graders."

Alice's five minute warning jolted me into action. I buzzed down to my classroom, dropped my books onto the desk, and surveyed the room. Five rows of five desks filled the stark, clean classroom. On the shelves by the windows, rows of textbooks stood in neat lines, their bindings revealing titles such as *Bright Peaks, Medieval Days and Ways*, and *The Spell of Words*. A colorful poster, tacked to the bulletin board in the front of the room, announced to the as yet uninitiated: "Books are Your Best Friends."

I turned to the blackboard, clean and fresh from a summer of solitude, and picked up a piece of chalk. In the crisp, clear script which I'd been practicing for the past three weeks, I wrote in large letters across the top of the blackboard: "Good Morning," and, under this cheerful greeting I wrote, "Mr. Rofes."

Sounds from the hallway announced the arrival of children. Sixth graders bounced into the classroom, wearing stylish back-to-school clothing, clutching new three-ring binders and un-scarred pencil cases. Happy to see one another, nervous at seeing me, the children alternated between unselfconscious greetings among themselves and courteous acknowledgement of the tall, bearded man at the front of the room. One short fellow with a head of dark, curly hair appeared obviously nervous about my presence but was unwilling to be intimidated by a mere adult. He approached me and, in a voice that squeaked as only an eleven-year-old boy on the brink of a voice change can squeak, asked abruptly, "Where do you want us to sit?"

Despite my valiant attempt to be fully prepared for the first day of school, this initial question thrown my way had never crossed my inexperienced mind. If he'd asked about writing on desks or the use of four-letter words, I'd have been ready with a response. As it was, I had to think fast. "For today," I answered, "I'd like you to sit wherever you'd like. We'll talk more about per-manent seating later this week."

The boy's face lit up and he turned and faced the dozen or so classmates already wandering around the classroom. "We can sit wherever we want!" he announced with glee. "He doesn't care where we sit today!" With that joyous message proclaimed, the children rushed about the room, staking out individual claims on specific desks. As some of the rowdier kids dropped their note-books onto the desks at the very back of the room, and some of the girls politely took seats in the front row, directly facing my desk, the curly-haired boy, Arthur, returned to continue our conversation.

"Last year," he squeaked, "Mr. Hamilton made us sit accord-ing to alphabetical order. He said that was the only fair way for everyone and that it wasn't a good idea for friends to sit next to each other in school. He'd keep one chair at the front of the room, where he'd make the kids sit if they weren't doing their work."

"That sounds like a fascinating arrangement, Arthur," I com-mented, attempting to sound fully noncommital and pro-fessional. "Perhaps once all the students have arrived we could try that arrangement with this class."

Realizing that he'd provided me with a model that was not in the best interests of the students, Arthur immediately continued. "I think that everyone would like it better if we chose our own seats. Especially since we're in the sixth grade now. Everyone would like you if you'd let us sit next to our friends."

"I am not here to win a popularity contest," I said in my serious teacher's voice. "I'm here to educate students, and whatever arrangement works best for teaching children to read and write and learn history is what arrangement we'll go with. For today, however, you may sit wherever you'd like." A cheer went up from the group. "All of you except Arthur," I said, pointing directly at him.

A look of surprise came over his face, fearful that he'd started off the school year on the wrong foot with this teacher who was twice his size. "I want you to sit up here, in the front row," I said, with a hint of a smile crossing my face. "I'm going to need a lot of advice today and you look like the one who can help me. I want you nearby to lend me a hand."

Beaming, he proudly took his possessions from the desk he'd claimed in the back row and moved to the front of the room, content with the knowledge that he'd already attained special status with the new teacher and the morning bell had yet to ring. I grabbed a handful of number two pencils from my desk and handed them to Arthur. "Please begin sharpening these pencils. We're going to need them today." My newly-acquired teacher's pet eagerly approached the sharpener and the grinding began.

It would have been difficult not to have a good first day of school. My twenty-five students appeared to be on their best behavior and ready to please. As I read down the class list, marveling to myself at the names of today's children (Jessica . . . Noah . . . Jesse . . . Monica . . . Alexandra . . . Heather . . . Gregory . . . Rachel . . .), my polite, shiny-faced children of suburban Boston families answered promptly with "present" or "here." I passed out books and materials, gave careful instructions and paced at the front of the room. While I was nervous and insecure,

I attempted to exude confidence, authority and clarity. I kept my eye on the list of tasks I'd penciled on the front page of my planning book, and proceeded from one to the other, until it was time for what I had listed as the "inspirational lecture," — the first pep talk of the year. Several friends had suggested this as a good way to "lay down the law," quickly and succinctly.

"Please close your books and put them away," I began in a quiet voice. "I want to be sure that you all listen to what I am going to tell you because it is important that we all understand some things at the beginning of our year together.

"You are all sixth graders now, the oldest class at the school. You will be graduating — hopefully — at the end of this school year, and going on to middle schools and junior high schools in the area. My goal for this year is to be sure that you have all the skills you will need to succeed in junior high school. Your teachers will provide you with everything you need to become strong, competent students — especially in reading, writing, public speaking, mathematics, history and geography. This is our job — the reason why we are here, at Shawmut Hills School, today.

"Each of you has your own job as well. It is your responsibility to make sure that you take your studies seriously and work diligently this year. You will need to aim for excellence and develop your study skills. If you feel unable to do the work, or if you are confused or unsure of yourself, ask me for help. I am more than happy to provide you with the extra attention that you may need. If I see that you are working up to your abilities, I will give you all the support that you need to succeed.

"However, if I find that you are lazy, or sloppy, or careless, or misbehaving, I will respond as well." Here many students averted their eyes from mine and gazed down at their desktops. "I will not accept papers that are poorly or carelessly written, homework that has been done at the last moment, excuses that are unsuitable to children at your age. I have high standards for all of you and I expect you to share these standards. If you do not, and if your work begins to suffer and your conduct begins to get difficult to manage, I will respond immediately. We are a sixth grade class — not a first grade class — and we have an example to set for ourselves and for the rest of the school.

"This does not mean that we won't have a good year here together, or that there is no place in the classroom for fun, humor or good times. I will promise you that I'll try to include interesting assignments, challenging activities, and enjoyable recreation as a part of our classroom life this year. But I will not forget the reason we are all here — to get a strong education — and I will not forget that I am the teacher and that it is my job to see that this is a successful year for you."

I finished the oration, turned and looked over the sea of little faces and was surprised to see the range of reactions from the children. Some sat at their desks, heads cowering, their eyes still averted. Others were sitting upright in their chairs, tall, proud, as if rising to the challenges of the speech. One girl, in the back of the room, looked as if I'd just told her that she had to complete a master's thesis before she'd graduate from sixth grade.

Realizing that this "To Sir, With Love" speech might well be misinterpreted, I decided to ask for immediate feedback. "Are there any questions about what I just discussed?" I asked, hoping to break the silence in the room with a bit more casual conversation than my speech. "I'd like to know your thoughts on these points and I'm happy to answer any questions that you might be wondering about."

I looked about the room and, surprisingly, a hand shot up immediately. A small, freckle-faced boy with a grin spreading across his face had the first question. "How much homework are we going to have this year?" he asked.

"That will depend on the particular night and on your individual skills at doing your homework," I responded. "How much homework did you have last year?"

"We never got more than an hour of homework," he answered.

From the grin on his face and the murmuring that rippled through the room, I knew that the others did not agree. I quickly asked if anyone remembered their fifth grade homework any differently than freckle-face described.

A girl in the front row, with her hair in pigtails tied with little pink ribbons at the ends, responded. "I remember it differently than Scotty just explained. We usually had about an hour and a half or two hours of homework last year," she said. "If we finished early, we had to do some work reading in a story book."

"I expect that this year, you will have between an hour an a half and two hours worth of homework each night," I explained. "There will be an emphasis on your writing, math, spelling and vocabulary. You will also have some memorizations, as well as your science and history homework. Are there any other questions?"

Curly-haired Arthur perked up. "What are we going to do for the Christmas play?" he asked.

I was amazed at the questions on the minds of these children. I had no significant experience working with sixth graders and hadn't realized their ingenuousness and ability to speak whatever was on their minds, however inappropriate at the moment. I had been warned, however, about the Christmas play. Performed each year by the sixth grade class at a special evening before Winter Vacation, the play was a greatly anticipated event for children entering their final year at the school. I was not prepared, however, to see this interest expressed on the first day of school.

"I'm looking over a few possibilities now," I lied, "but I won't be able to tell you about them until the middle of October. Of course, I'll be open to any suggestions that you might have, but I'd like to hold those until next week."

A red-haired, red-cheeked girl in the back of the room raised her hand. "Like, who are you, and where do you come from? Where did you used to teach, and stuff like that?" she asked in an especially whiney voice that I knew had the potential to drive me crazy by December.

Who was I? Where was I from? What should I tell these kids about my life?

I was already too aware of the differences between myself and my students to answer this question casually. Whereas these were the children of successful, upper-middle-class professionals, I knew that much of my biography wouldn't seem exciting to these kids. Could I compare their days at the small, proper Shawmut Hills School, complete with its playing fields, woods, and swimming pool with my days at suburban public schools, such as North Ridge School, where I attended sixth grade along with the children of other Jewish, Italian and Irish commuters who drove an hour and half each morning into Manhattan? Should I tell them about my current residence, in a household of six friends in working-class Somerville and, unlike their own parents, none of us were married? Should I explain that I'd gotten this job as a one-year replacement for the sixth grade teacher who was on sabbatical through my adviser at Harvard whose daughter was in the school's fourth grade class — and that I'd accepted the job, and its salary of $7,000 a year, because I'd been unsure of my future, aimlessly drifting without career ambitions?

A part of me wanted to be outrageous — and right here and now simply announce, "I'm a 22-year-old Jewish homosexual. Have you ever seen a Jew before? What about a homosexual? Do you know what that word means, little children? Can you spell 'homosexual?' "

I shifted back to reality and chose a safer route. "I recently graduated from Harvard College," I told them, knowing that this information would impress their families if it found its way home, "and I did my student teaching at the high school level at a private school west of here —"

"Which one?" asked the red-cheeked girl, her eager eyes indicating a personal interest in my response.

"The Oxford School," I answered. "Some of you may have heard of it."

"My sister goes there," she announced, "and when I'm in ninth grade, I'm going to go there too."

"I enjoyed teaching there and perhaps some time you and I could talk about the school," I responded, sensing a way to change the subject away from personal probings of my biography. "For now, are there any other questions before we move into snack time?"

"I have another one," came the voice from the back of the room. Monica, the red-headed bundle of energy again had her hand waving wildly. "Are you married?" she asked, this time with an embarrassed grin on her lips and her face blushing redder than ever.

I tried not to let my surprise show on my face, but I'm sure that I also started to blush. It was fine to discuss homework, Christmas plays, and seating arrangements with these kids. But I'd assumed that teaching eleven-year-olds would leave me safe from such direct questioning of my personal life. I had been assured by knowledgeable friends that, at this grade level, I needn't worry about creating a fictional life for myself. Kids didn't care about these kinds of things.

I was wrong.

Pulling my thoughts together quickly, I replied simply, "No, I'm not married." Then I added, "But I'm younger than I look and I don't expect to be married for a while." Honest enough, I thought to myself, however misleading.

"How old are you?" Monica pressed on.

"Now you're getting *too* personal," I answered insistently. "Let's move into snack time, now."

The remainder of the day was a jumble of activity. We reviewed spelling rules, worked through an assessment of vocabulary level, discussed penmanship expectations, and I presented our first writing assignment. We walked through a practice fire drill ("Everyone hold hands with your buddy!") and I explained the schedule for the week. Lunchtime found me seated at the head of a table of twelve children spanning third through sixth grade, serving hamburgers and mashed potatoes and reminding children to put their napkins on their laps and use their forks rather than their fingers. During recess, the children played outdoors, supervised by several teachers, while the rest of the staff retreated into the faculty room, where we swapped first-day-of-school stories and found the collective energy to survive the next two hours.

It became clear to me that I would have less difficulty gaining control of the classroom than I'd anticipated. One of my greatest fears had been that I would be uncomfortable asserting authority. On one hand, I felt that the fact that I presented expectations in a clear fashion made it easier to maintain control of twenty-five children. On the other hand, I could not deny that being a man, and a large man at that, gave me the upper hand with these children. As curly-haired Arthur later told me, "You're a big guy with a big, dark beard and a deep voice. Next to all of us little kids, you look like some kind of Bigfoot monster. We'd be crazy to mess around with you."

By the time it was three o'clock, I felt fine about my first day and eager to go to sleep for a week. After I dismissed the class, several students came up to the front of the room.

One was the freckle-faced boy with the big smile. Scott was again beaming and said to me, "Do I really have to finish that paper for tomorrow? I'm not too good at writing . . ."

"Yes," I stated firmly. "The paper is due tomorrow and I expect a good job from you Scott."

Scott groaned, made more excuses, and then, still grinning, ran out of the room, his book bag over his shoulder.

Ann, the girl with pigtails, was waiting also. "I want to show you my notebook, so you can let me know if it is okay for this year," she said coyly. Ann took out her three-ring binder with a photograph of the cast of "Welcome Back, Kotter" on the cover, and talked me through each of the sections. "This part's for math work," she said, "and this is for writing papers. Here's where I'll put my spelling papers, and this section is for science." Then she looked up at me, giggling flirtatiously. "Do I get an A?"

"I don't give grades for notebooks, Ann," I responded, attempting to deflect her attempt to flirt with the teacher. "But your book looks very nice and I appreciate your taking the time to show it to me."

As the last of the students departed through the door, a

woman poked her head into the classroom. I walked over to the door and came face to face with a tall, middle-aged woman in a gingham print dress and heels.

"Hello," I said. "Are you looking for someone?"

"Are you Mr. Rofes?" she asked. "I'm Mrs. Green, Amy's mother." I quickly attempted to match Amy's name with the faces which had been surrounding me all day. She continued, "I just wanted to come in and wish you well. I know this is an awfully big class to have, especially for a new teacher like yourself. But they're a good bunch of kids — especially Amy and her friends."

"I very much enjoyed my first day, Mrs. Green, and I feel quite capable of keeping control of the class." I began closing up my papers and materials on my desk and tucking them into my backpack.

"Do you live in Shawmut Hills?" she asked. "I've never seen you around town before."

"No, I don't live here," I responded. "I live in Somerville, near Cambridge."

"Oh," she said, a bit surprised. "Most of our teachers live over here in the suburbs. Do your children go to the Somerville schools?"

"I don't have any children," I said, finishing closing up my backpack. I stood up and looked her in the eye.

"Are you married?" she asked unabashedly.

"No, I am not," I stated, annoyed that, for the second time today, I should have to face a question about my marital status. Obviously, this was on everyone's mind in Shawmut Hills.

"Oh," she again said, surprised. "Well, that's *very* interesting to know. It's been very nice to meet you. I'm sure that I'll see you again soon. After all," she continued, "I *am* your class mother. That means that you can call on me whenever you need me. I'm in the school directory, under Green, Annette Green. Do give me a call."

"Thank you very much, Mrs. Green," I said, hoisting my pack onto my shoulder.

"Annette," she insisted. "Please call me Annette." And with a wave of her hand, she turned, smiled and left the room.

— 2 —

I'd awaken at 6:30 each morning that fall, shower, dress and grab breakfast before running to catch the bus to work. After changing buses in Harvard Square, I'd travel twenty minutes and be dropped at the foot of Shawmut Hill. A ten minute trudge through autumn leaves would take me to maple-lined Shawmut Hill Lane and the Shawmut Hills School.

I quickly established an open, direct, and occasionally challenging relationship with the school's headmistress, Miss Beatrice Clarkson. Despite the tumult of the sixties and the excitement of experimental education in the seventies, Shawmut Hills School managed to retain a headmistress who walked out of the thirties. Miss Clarkson was grey-haired, bespectacled, and had the perfect posture that comes out of an era when girls attended cloistered finishing schools and were instructed in etiquette and posture maintenance. She spoke in a clear, controlled monotone and had mastered the art of looking a person directly in the eye without revealing a hint of personal emotion or human warmth. Because she had served the school for 20 years, much of the younger staff of the school considered her to be a relic out-of-touch with contemporary issues in education. In the faculty room, the only place in the building teachers had the time to discuss such matters, she was alternately described as a prig, tyrant, tough cookie and a witch.

I viewed Miss Clarkson as a woman set firmly in the tradition of the New England spinster school-marms — those women who flouted traditional expectations by entering the field of education, never marrying, and directing their energies into their students. During a period when few career options were open to women, these teachers managed to forge a path as independent women. I found it easy to respect these women, although I did not always find it easy to respect Miss Clarkson.

On entering the school each morning, we were expected to sign an attendance sheet at the front desk. Miss Clarkson would be standing there, usually in a modest cardigan sweater with a flowered brooch on the lapel, a dark, drab skirt that reached well below the knees, and what looked like orthopedic shoes. As each teacher arrived she was ready with a cheery "Good morning" and a word of advice or reminder for the day. This simple ritual — while lasting only about 30 seconds — had the effect of jolting a teacher from the last blinks of sleepiness into the realities of a school day.

One morning in October, I found myself running a bit late. Having missed the bus in Harvard Square, I arrived at school at 8:05, precisely five minutes ahead of the children. I pushed through the front door, signed in quickly, and was relieved to find Miss Clarkson away from her usual post. As I elbowed my way through the crowd in the front lobby, Miss Clarkson's secretary called out to me, "Oh Mr. Rofes — Miss Clarkson would like to see you in her office."

Such a request had never before interrupted my morning ritual. As I changed directions and headed down the short corridor into Miss Clarkson's office, my mind raced with paranoid possibilities. Was I too strict with a student? Too lenient? Had I given too much homework last night? Did a student complain about the memorizations I was assigning?

Or was it something personal — something about me? While I had felt that I had quickly become quite skilled at sidestepping questions about my marital status, lurking within me was the fear that I was going to be "found out." When I'd avoided the secretary's well-intentioned efforts to fix me up on a blind date with one of her friends, I felt glaringly exposed. Had my sidestepping blown my cover?

I glanced down at my clothing. Did I look too faggy today? I thought I had been careful not to wear what I called "give-away" clothing — shirts that screamed "This boy's a queer!" and pants that were too tight and too fashionable to allow anyone to think they would be worn by a straight man. My mind raced with possible scenarios.

I popped my head into Miss Clarkson's office. "Did you want to see me?" I asked gingerly.

"Yes, I did. Thank you, Eric," she said in her crisp, formal tone of voice. "Come in and close the door for a minute."

As I closed the door, I imagined the worst. A confidential conference with the head of the school could only mean one thing. I took my seat, sat with my best posture, and looked up at Miss Clarkson.

She began. "It's been brought to my attention that you have been telling the students about — how shall we put this — your *unconventional* living situation."

My eyes darted away from hers and shot out the window to the playing fields and autumn leaves of the school grounds. My mind leaped immediately to a conversation I'd had with my students just a week earlier. As I grappled with my weak memory of what was actually said and the context within which the questions appeared, Miss Clarkson continued.

"I want you to know that the feedback I've received concerning your teaching has, up until this point, been only positive. Parents are pleased with your high expectations for the boys and girls, and feel that you are presenting a challenging and exciting program. The children also seem to like you a great deal and, as you well know, this is a curcial part of the teacher-child relationship at this age.

"I am concerned, however, as are several parents who took

the time out of their busy schedules to telephone the school, about the freedom with which you seem to talk about your — how shall I put this — personal life outside of school."

It was time to respond. "All I've been doing is answering the kids' questions. They asked me last week if I were living with a girlfriend. When I told them that I wasn't they immediately assumed I lived alone. It was at that point, that I told them that I lived with several other people in a collective house in Soverville."

Miss Clarkson looked at me with a determined and unchanged look on her face. She continued, "What you do not seem to understand, Eric, is that we live in a conservative community, and many parents would be shocked to hear that you live with other adults — including women to whom you are not married — in what they would assume to be a 1960's commune. It is even more difficult for these parents, when you impart that information to their children, whom they are attempting to raise with their own moral visions. Many of the children in this school come from religious homes which would not allow for such living situations."

"Don't you think that it is important for children's questions to be answered honestly?" I asked quietly, staring at the floor.

"We are here to teach children to read and write and do their mathematics," she began. "We are not here to answer all their questions about the world, nor are we here to become friends with the students. I am aware that many new teachers — like yourself — arrive at teaching without a firm understanding of the proper relationship one is to have with one's students, and I view it as my responsibility to keep you informed of appropriate conduct and discussion between teacher and child. It simply is not acceptable for a teacher to discuss his personal life with the children and this is something you will come to understand more fully, as you become a more experienced teacher."

My mind raced to my own education and all those teachers who had managed to refer to their husbands and wives and children during an unrelated history lesson; to the party we threw for Miss

Barth in fourth grade when she became Mrs. Brendel. I thought of the wedding rings worn by other teachers at Shawmut Hills and the way these rings served as a silent flaunting of their marital status. I remembered how everyone at Shawmut Hills — children, parents, faculty — within the first weeks of school all appeared determined to pry into my love life. As long as the personal life was conventional — as long as the "family" in question was a traditional nuclear family — I was sure that teachers would hear no objections. Once our lives fell outside the narrow dictates of Shawmut Hills' society, they became inappropriate for discussion.

Miss Clarkson glanced down at her watch. "The bell will ring in two minutes," she said. "I see no reason to discuss this matter further. I've assured parents that it will not happen again. You'd better go and prepare for your morning classes."

And, with that dismissal, Miss Clarkson arose from her chair and ushered me out of the office.

I began that day with a vague sense of relief — relieved that Miss Clarkson hadn't gotten angrier about what appeared to be a clear violation of the school's teacher-student ethics, and relieved to hear that I was getting good reviews from the parents and the children. I vowed to keep my personal life far from the classroom and behave myself. With such high risks potentially involved in providing information about myself to the children, it was probably easier for everyone involved, including me, to keep things distant and, in Miss Clarkson's term, "professional."

This lack of "professionalism" was not my only problem as a new teacher. My inexperience combined with my idealism to bring about several embarrassing educational "bloopers." When I passed out my first list of spelling words, the kids reacted with surprise. Not only were words such as "euphemism" and "metamorphosis" difficult to spell, but my students had no idea what the words meant — even after reading the dictionary definition. Having had little prior contact with eleven year olds, I had created the list from a mental approximation of their vocabulary level. The problem was exacerbated by my stubborn refusal to give in to the children's request for more appropriate words. This brought on nasty phone calls from parents, snide remarks from the children, and a command meeting with the school's language arts specialist. I survived that trial, but I quickly found a grade-level spelling index to use in creating future lists.

There was also the time I walked into the classroom to find most of the students engaged in a game of keep-away, throwing the baseball cap of the class scapegoat around the room as he ran to and fro, tears streaming down his cheeks. My temper was immediately triggered and I unleashed a fury of words in my loudest voice. Calling the perpetrators of this prank by name, I categorized them as "evil, bad people" who took "sick, sadistic pleasure" from this kind of torture. Only after about five minutes of this sort of castigating did I calm down enough to notice Miss Clarkson with a look of horror upon her face, standing in the doorway of the classroom with a group of prospective parents in tow.

Despite my errant ways, I was somehow managing to feel a bit like a professional educator. While most of the faculty looked on me as a novice teacher, I worked hard to insure that my students and my classroom appeared to reflect some level of competency at maintaining discipline, creating an exciting and academically sound program, and upholding the good name of Shawmut Hills School.

My regular meetings and luncheons with Alice, the librarian, kept me apprised of my position in the school and helped me mold a reputation for myself as a cooperative colleague. As is often the case, the secretaries and librarians were the information center of the school. And, as any teacher can tell you, in the educational field, information is power.

One afternoon, over a lunch of soup and sandwiches in the school's faculty room, Alice and I discussed my position in the school's faculty hierarchy. Alice was a short, plump and energetic woman who most of the day could be found in the recesses of the library, rifling through cartons of newly-arrived books, mounting displays of literature to capture the imaginations of the children, or sitting with a group of first-graders reading *Make Way For Ducklings* with animation and excitement. As the school's earth mother, Alice was always there to lend a sympathetic ear. After patiently listening to your problems, she'd allow her bifocals to slip slowly down her nose, look at you eyeball to eyeball and say "I see the problem but I think I may also see a solution." She'd then present you with just the right combination of common sense and good humor. If there were one person who maintained the spirit and sanity of the Shawmut Hills School faculty, it was Alice the Librarian.

I stared across the lunch table at Alice, who was peering at me over her spectacles, thinking seriously. "You know, Eric," she told me, "as the only classroom teacher in this school who's a man, you're in a pretty unique position — both in terms of the rest of the staff and in terms of Beatrice and her school board."

After a fifteen year tenure in the school, Alice was one of the few faculty members who was permitted to call Miss Clarkson by her first name. This gave her a stature among teachers that was difficult to define but lent her a great deal of respect and credence.

"I'm not sure what you're getting at, Alice," I said. "What kind of 'unique position' do you think I'm in?" I had been all too aware that aside from the boys' gym teacher, I was the only man teaching in the school. I had not been aware, however, that this gave me any kind of special status.

She continued. "The school often has had a man teaching sixth grade and, traditionally, this person has had the greatest difficulty getting along with Beatrice. I'm not sure whether it is the nature of being a man, or being the teacher of the oldest children in the school, or because she feels judged by your work because of the achievement tests your kids will take in the spring. In any case, Beatrice frequently has been quite circumspect with the sixth grade teacher and an unusual kind of power dynamic has emerged. From my point of view, it has always appeared to be quite a competitive situation.

"Additionally," she said, taking a big bite out of the grilled cheese, "you'll notice that the rest of the teachers look to you for championing their causes and standing up to Beatrice. I'm not sure why this is so, but I see it happening already, so I thought I'd warn you. You seem to be the ideal person for that sort of work but, before you placed yourself in that position, I wanted to be sure that you were aware of the possible ramifications of such 'subversive' activity..."

This did not sound good. "I want you to know, Alice, that I have no interest in taking on Miss Clarkson or challenging her on issues related to education. I mean, I just graduated from college. I'm probably the last person in the school to be able to discuss educational philosophy. Plus, I really don't want to be in controversial positions at a job I'm only at for one year while the *real* sixth grade teacher's on sabbatical. It's hard enough already teaching twenty-five kids and dealing with their parents."

"Eat your soup, Eric, before it gets cold," Alice said with a smile. "Whether or not you want to be in this position, you're in it. In all my years here, some have fared well and some haven't in your position. Shawmut Hills is run in a very simple hierarchy — Beatrice is at the top and all of us are down below. There is little sharing of power and responsibility and no way to avoid allowing her to be the ultimate authority. We're powerless on matters such as hiring and firing. If you give her a rough time, she could make life miserable for you."

Alice pushed her tray back, forced her bifocals up the bridge of her nose and looked at me. "You're in a good position, I guess. Being a new teacher, fresh out of Harvard, with all these liberal views of education. I can tell already that Beatrice isn't quite sure what to make of you and is suspicious of your teaching and your style. Except for a few mistakes, you've been able to get the parents and kids into the palm of your hand and this must be a big relief to her. She doesn't have to worry about a whole lot of complaints about the children's last year at the school being what we refer to as "less than challenging" or being overly-academic and boring. I'd place my bets that she wants to keep you on her good side, as long as you continue to get the rave reviews and as long as you don't threaten her power too much. Plus, you should be aware of the fact that there's a real possibility that your predecessor won't be returning next year. You could be in line for a permanent position, if that's what you want."

"Thanks for telling me all of this, Alice," I said. "I guess it's good for me to hear this, but why are you telling me now?"

"Word is out that you're doing some controversial things in your classroom — using drama and art as a part of the Middle Ages class, threatening to do a Christmas play that tones down the Christianity, talking to the kids about those folks you live with in Somerville — and that you're getting your share of flak from Beatrice. People are bound to be a little jealous and a little nervous at the same time. I've got to get back to the library now, but I just wanted to be sure that you're aware of what's being said about you and that you approach these matters with your eyes open." Alice started to stack our dishes onto her tray.

"Also," she said, "my kid brother made me promise to keep my eye out for you this year and, while we certainly had our share of sibling rivalry during our younger years, I do try to keep my promises to my brother Ronald." With a wink of an eye, Alice got up, took our trays, and slipped into the hallway.

Ron LeBlanc, Alice's kid brother, was — in a small way — responsible for getting me the job at Shawmat Hills School. Ron was a college classmate of mine who had gone to the school as a child. I heard about the opening at the school from my Harvard advisor whose daughter was currently in the school's fourth grade. I sent in my resume at his urging. When Ron heard that I had applied for a job at the school, he told his sister to put in a good word for me. Whether she did or not, I'll never know, but I was aware that in the world of independent schools in the Boston area, connections were the glue that cemented job hirings. I had assumed that the LeBlanc family connection had aided my entry into the school.

Another factor related to all of this was that I had maintained a mad crush on Ron during most of my senior year at college. On discovering that Ron — the thin, bearded art student with the El

Greco face that had mesmerized me through Fine Arts lectures — was gay (we shared a mutual friend for a few months and, late one evening, we ran into one another on his doorstep; Ron leaving as I was arriving) — I immediately spirited myself into his life. During the winter and spring of my final term at Harvard, this adolescent crush obsessed me and led me to Ron's off-campus apartment for late-night study sessions. Much to my disappointment, a romance never developed, but friendship did and it was through this friendship that I linked up with the job at Shawmut Hills.

Ron and his sister had a relationship filled with the typical tensions felt between older sisters and younger brothers with over a decade separating the two. I wondered if Alice assumed I was gay because Ron and I were friends. My own apprehensions about mixing my two lives led me to guard this information carefully from her.

Ron was, therefore, the only person who knew Shawmut Hills to whom I could talk about being gay there. Ron had filled me in on the internal politics of the school, as well as the history of Miss Clarkson's tenure before I had arrived to teach my first class. His advice was to keep quiet about my personal life — although he had suspicions about spinster headmistresses — and to avoid all controversy. As Ron said to me once, "Shawmut Hills is a conservative community. Do you think these people want a fag teaching their kids?"

I took Ron's advice through the early days of the fall and felt fully capable of dealing with the day-to-day responsibilities of my job and avoiding confrontations that would pull me even inches out of the closet. This was generally easy, as one learns quickly to avoid particular conversations or to glance quickly at one's watch in the faculty room, and get up saying, "I've got a lesson to teach," when certain threatening issues are raised. Retaining some small degree of integrity, I knew I wanted to avoid playing "Monday Morning Pronouns," a game that involved telling colleagues about my "hot date" over the weekend, only changing the "he" to a "she." I regularly struggled to find a comfortable peace with this awkward situation.

During the waning days of October, my precarious peace was disturbed by my twelve-year-old students. The class was sitting in small groups of five or six children, reading books aloud to one another. I was seated quietly at my desk, grading spelling tests — not my favorite activity.

All of a sudden, one group broke into simultaneous hysterical laughter. They were laughing in the embarrassed way that many teachers are familiar with, when students turn red in the face and refuse to look you directly in the eye.

"What's so funny?" I asked, coming over to the group.

All eyes turned the other way. More giggling. Finally, one brave soul raised her voice: "Mr. Rofes, do you know what the word 'gay' means?"

Stalling for time, I responded, "Please read me the sentence, Ann."

She brazenly tossed her pigtails over her shoulders, looked in her book and read, "The gay colors of the peasants' clothing made the festival a joyous sight." More laughter.

"Yes, Ann, in that sentence, 'gay' means bright, vivid, pretty blues and yellows and reds," I answered with a straight face.

Ann looked at me. Then she turned to her peers, wide-eyed in amazement. "He doesn't know what it means! Mr. Rofes doesn't know what 'gay' means!" And then she looked at me right in the eye and, in a serious tone similar to the voice I'd heard adults use in telling a youngster that babies, in fact, do not come from a stork, Ann let me in on the big secret. "It doesn't only mean that. It means something else, too."

"Oh? And what's that?" I asked innocently.

There was no way that Ann or anyone else was going to tell me. Finally, it came to me all of a sudden.

"Oh," I said with an obvious show of surprise. "You mean 'gay' like 'homosexual.' Men who are attracted to men and women who are attracted to women. I don't think that's what the author meant in this case."

A stunned look came over the whole class. By now everyone was listening. I felt called upon to continue. "I don't think that gay people are anything for you to laugh at. You might not know any gay people yourselves, but that's no reason to be afraid or prejudiced. It's something that may be confusing or scary to you now, but when you're older, I expect you'll understand a lot better."

With that, I asked the children to return to their reading and — with a sense of relief for us all — their little eyes reverted to their books.

As I returned to grading papers, my mind immediately raced with paranoid fantasies. I kicked myself for being unable to avoid controversial issues in the classroom. If Miss Clarkson was concerned about talk of my housemates with the children, today's discussion would infuriate her. I must find a way, I told myself, to avoid these risks. As I sat there, attempting to work, I felt wave upon wave of fear and anger wash over me — anger at Miss Clarkson, at my situation, and finally, at myself.

What was I doing in this situation? When I followed the best of my beliefs and moral instincts and spoke honestly to the kids about the issues on their minds, I felt terrified that Miss Clarkson would discover my transgression. When I sidestepped their questions or lied to the kids to avoid controversy, I felt overwhelmed by guilt at my lack of backbone.

What the hell was I doing in this situation?

I was meeting my best friend for dinner that night and, although Paul was not gay, he was a schoolteacher and I needed his advice on how I handled the matter. I had met Paul when I joined the Men's Childcare Collective, a group of men who worked either as daycare teachers, childcare volunteers, or schoolteachers. We met regularly to debate issues related to kids, provide childcare services for feminist events, visit local shelters for battered women and take the kids on short excursions to nearby playgrounds. Paul and I immediately became fast friends, sharing a cynical sense of humor. I admired his gentle nature, as well as his skills in working with children with special needs.

We met over dinner at the Golden Horde, a Chinese restaurant in Cambridge. As Paul poured the tea, I raised my dilemma.

"I'm just not sure I handled the situation right," I said in a strained voice. "What do you think?"

Paul's dark brown eyes looked up at me. I knew that I appeared flustered. "Well, whether you handled it well or not seems less important to me than how upset this has made you feel."

"I mean, Christ, Paul, does every children's book writer have to put the word 'gay' into every chapter?"

"Now come on, you're exaggerating a bit."

"No I'm not. Children skip 'gaily'; spring is a 'gay' season, the ribbons are always bright and 'gay.' Is there a conspiracy out there to humiliate gay teachers?"

Paul drank his tea slowly and fiddled with his chopsticks. He stared at me for a moment, thoughtfully raking his fingers through his curly black beard. "I think you handled the matter pretty well. Remember that the kid brought up the question, not you. All you did was answer her. Right?"

"Terrific! All I did was tell the whole class of sixth graders about what homos are."

"You were just answering a question."

"But that's what Clarkson thinks I do a little too much of."

"What's that?"

"Answer questions. It seems as if administrators don't want teachers to answer controversial questions. Education is supposed to be free from this thing they call personal bias. What a load of bullshit!"

Momentarily distracted by the arrival of the lo mein and egg foo yung piping hot, Paul hesitated and then responded.

"Risks are a part of teaching. Unfortunately, too many good teachers are reluctant to take the risks because of reactions from administrators and teachers."

"And because teaching jobs are hard to find these days."

"You're right. If you're doing a good job, Eric, I'll bet that a little talk with the kids about homosexuality isn't going to make such a big deal. Because it's such a hot issue, I'll bet they don't even tell their parents about it. Kids in sixth grade are often too embarrassed to discuss anything at all about sex with their folks."

Paul reached over and stuck his chopsticks into my fried rice. "I think I know what might really be on your mind," he said quietly.

"What?"

"You feel guilty because you didn't tell them that you're gay. Is that it?"

"Bullshit! I don't feel that way at all."

"Don't you feel just a little bit dishonest and think that you copped out by dealing with the question the way you did?"

"I don't think I could have come out to them. Not in *that* school."

"Uh-huh," Paul nodded.

"Not being a *new* teacher."

"Uh-huh," he nodded again.

"Not with *twelve*-year-old kids."

Again Paul nodded his head in agreement and stared at me. I stabbed my chopsticks into Paul's foo yung and continued speaking rapidly.

"Plus, I think it's absolutely crazy for any teacher to come out to kids that young. Kids can't understand what it means. It confuses them. They're too busy dealing with pimples and pubic hair."

"That's probably keeping them pretty busy," Paul agreed.

I kept going. "I wonder what some gay teachers get out of being openly gay with their kids. I think it's some kind of selfish decision that could screw the kids up for life. I would never want to reveal that kind of information to my students, especially — "

"Hold it, hold it, hold it," Paul interrupted. "I don't see why you're getting so defensive about this. All I asked was if you didn't feel ambivalent about not telling the kids that you're gay. From what I just saw, you over-reacted a tiny bit."

I sat back quietly for a moment and played with the remains of my food.

"I guess I have some mixed feelings about the position that I'm in."

"I'm sorry. I don't want you to feel that I think you should be coming out of the closet at Shawmut Hills School."

"What do you think?"

"In general ... I think it's important for your own sake to recognize the mixed feelings you have and be ready to deal with them when they arise."

"I'll tell you, Paul. This isn't going to keep happening. I couldn't take it."

"I'm sure this won't be the last time. People who think that homosexuality is a subject that doesn't come up with kids — be they ten years old or eighteen years old — haven't worked with kids over the past decade. From the fag jokes to the lezzie comments to outright questions, to insults, terms papers, current events and psychology texts, homosexuality creeps into the schools these days, no matter what some educators claim."

By the time the fortune cookies arrived, I was a lot calmer. Paul handed me the dish with two cookies. "Pick one," he said.

I chose the larger one, cracked it open, and read the fortune to myself.

"What does it say?" Paul asked curiously.

I read the writing that appeared on the little pink slip. "It says, 'Among all the lucky, you are the chosen one.' " I paused for a moment. "Great," I said to Paul. "Chosen for what?"

Paul knew what he was talking about when it came to children raising the subject of homosexuality. On lunch duty that fall, I'd hear kids insult each other on the soccer field with "You faggot!" On seeing a classmate's pink shirt, freckle-faced Scott asked with a big, mischievous grin, "What are you, gay or something?" And the girls were not exempt from this kind of baiting. Two girls in a close friendship would be called "those lezzies," to the titters of the other girls.

One day, Monica came up to my desk before school. She was one of my favorite students — always filled with energy, goodwill, and lots of gossip. Her thick, red hair was always neatly trimmed and adorned with colorful ribbons and decorative hairclips. This morning, however, her usually pink, smiling face had taken on the expression of a widow.

"I'm burning all of my Olivia Newton-John records after school today," she announced proudly.

I looked up from my planning book. "What did you say, Monica?" I asked.

"I said, I'm burning my Olivia Newton-John records after school today."

I put down my book. "Why do you want to do that?" I asked.

"Because she's gay," Monica answered. She then went on to tell a story that her older sister had presented at the breakfast table that morning. The sister claimed that — during the evening before on the Johnny Carson show — Olivia Newton-John was a guest and Carson prodded her about her love life and her boy-friend. After resisting the questions prying into her personal life and sidestepping Carson's boorishness, Olivia allegedly announced that, yes, she was in love. In fact, her lover was in the audience at that very moment. Carson asked that the camera be turned onto the audience and the lover identify himself. Olivia then, in Monica's wide-eyed account, stepped off the stage and into the arms of a woman. At which point, they both gave Carson what Monica termed 'the finger' and left the studio.

"That sounds like quite a story," I said, controlling my own inner excitement at this news. "Why does that make you want to burn your records?"

Monica looked at me as if I'd just asked her the stupidest question in the world. "Well, because she's gay. When they're women they call them a thespian," she informed me. "That means she likes women and not men. That's sick."

"The word you're looking for is 'lesbian,' " I corrected her. " 'Thespian' is a person involved in acting and drama. 'Lesbian' is a gay woman. In any case, how does this affect the records that I know you've enjoyed?" Monica had made it clear at several occasions earlier in the fall that Newton-John was her favorite singer.

"All those songs are meaningless now. They're all lies. She's singing songs to men, but they're really to women. Look at that song 'Sam' she sings," Monica insisted, becoming a music sleuth. "My sister says the song is really about a woman named 'Saman-tha.' I can't sing that song now."

By now, a crowd had gathered and joined into the discussion. Arthur added his wisdom, "She's a lousy singer, anyway," he said in his squeaky voice. "I don't know why you didn't burn the records a long time ago."

Amy Green, a girl with a mouthful of braces, chimed in. "Well, Monica, I like her records too, and I don't care if she's sing-ing that song to a girl or a boy. I can sing it to a boy if I want to. She's still my favorite singer."

Monica seemed backed into a corner and needed a way out. Amy continued, "Why don't you keep the records and just pretend that someone else is singing them. Then you can enjoy the music and forget all about Olivia. Just put them into another album jacket — like Debbie Boone."

That seemed to provide Monica with what she needed. "I think I'll do that," Monica said. "And, anyway, my sister told me that I was crazy for wanting to burn albums. She said that if I had to burn all the albums of all the gay singers, I'd lose half my col-lection. Even Johnny Mathis!"

The bell rang, the kids hurried to take their seats, and I began the vocabulary lesson for the day.

The more experience I gained in the classroom, the more ap-parent it became that working with the kids' attitudes about homosexuality, gender distinctions and same-sex relationships was crucial to their development. Only my fear and my isolation in the school held me back from more aggressive work in these areas. As long as I felt alone and unsupported within the school, it was impossible to make any truly courageous moves. Alice was always there in the library, providing support and a helping hand, but we avoided discussing my personal life and I was led to be-lieve that Ron's erratic relationship with his sister revolved, to some extent, around his homosexuality. I wasn't about to set at risk my one solid relationship in the school by coming out of the closet.

Of course, there were other teachers and staff members with whom I felt a sense of camaraderie: the French teacher who was wonderful with the kids and looked like a model off the pages of *Vogue* magazine; the woman who taught my kids science and mathematics, who was engaged in her own battles with the head-mistress regarding teaching style and curriculum; and the creative woman who specialized in drama and art and was a breath of fresh air in this dowdy, middle-of-the-road school. I did not feel close enough, however, to any of these people to share the specific aspects of my personal life. Even when the French teacher threw a Halloween party, during the second month of school, and invited me to attend, I brought along a female college friend as a cover to help me through the social situation. As it happened, our hostess was urbane enough to know several gay people and I felt caught between maintaining my cover with her and flirting with some of her attractive male friends.

As the autumn passed by, and school bulletin boards shed their orange, brown and red leaves for snowflakes roughly cut from white construction paper by small, untrained hands, I began to feel more confident in my position. Teachers at Shawmut Hills received a strange kind of respect from parents. Since school finances were an open book, I suppose that parents felt they had to be overly thankful to a teacher whom they felt was doing a decent job with their child, lest another job offer come along mid-year and spirit the teacher away to a better salary.

One day, as I was strolling through Shawmut Hills' down-town area — a small strip of shops, markets and banks that was architecturally designed to appear as a small, New England town while, in fact, it was the heart of suburbia — I ran into Mrs. Sabinsky. She was the mother of a student in my class and quite active in the school both as a class mother and as a board member. She was, at that moment, engaged in a conversation in front of the A&P with Annette Green.

"Mr. Rofes, how nice to see you today," Mrs. Green exclaimed, taking my hand. "Or should I say, Eric. I hear only wonderful things from Amy and her friends about the school year. I can't wait until parent conference time. We do have *so* much to talk about."

"That's good to hear," I said, in a brusque tone. I looked over to Mrs. Sabinsky. She smiled, knowingly. "Nice to see you as well, Mrs. Sabinsky," I said, returning her friendly smile.

Annette interrupted before Mrs. Sabinsky had a chance to respond. "I have to take the girls to ballet class now, so sorry I can't stop and chat. We'll talk soon, I'm sure, Eric," she said. "And Linda, give me a call tomorrow. Bye-bye!" With that, she turned and hurried off.

Mrs. Sabinsky looked up at me and shifted her grocery bag in her arms. "Mr. Rofes," she said in a warm voice. "Do you have a second? I suppose I should arrange a conference to speak with you about this, but if you have some time now, I'd really like to have a little chat."

I let my backpack, laden with books, slip off my shoulder and placed it down at my feet. "I'm in no rush," I said in my most commodious, I'm-only-here-to-serve-you voice. "Why don't we stop into Friendly's for a cup of coffee?"

Making sure I properly held the door for her I entered the restaurant with Mrs. Sabinsky and sat at a booth at a window. After we had ordered our coffee, she looked up at me.

"I don't really know how to say this, but, because you seem so sensitive to the kids, and they adore you so much, I'm hoping you can help Stewart with a problem that he's having with some of the children outside of school."

I couldn't imagine what she was talking about. Her son Stewart was popular, bright, and the leader of the athletic boys' group in the class. I tried to imagine what problems other children could be causing this boy.

She continued. "It seems that he and Jack have really become strong friends this year. They're always together — at soccer games, or playing football, or just going to the stores. We're very pleased that their friendship has continued to develop this year since they're so much alike and, as you know, Jack's mother Estelle and I are very good friends.

"The problem seems to be that other kids are making fun of their friendship — calling them names, you know? In the beginning, I don't think this bothered the boys, but recently I've noticed that Stewart seems a little reluctant to invite Jack over. I just want to be sure that a little bit of nasty name calling doesn't destroy a very nice and very special friendship."

I gazed out the window as the sun was disappearing behind the town library. I hadn't noticed any problems between Stewart and Jack and the other children, although I had certainly noticed their friendship and felt positively about the influence it had on both of the boys. I was surprised to hear that other kids were baiting them, since they were clearly the strongest, most popular boys and, I suspect, it was a bit risky for the others to mock them.

"Have you talked to Stewart about it?" I asked.

Mrs. Sabinsky looked down at the table. "Now that's the problem. Stewart won't talk to me about anything serious. You know — adolescent rebellion against the mother and all that. And his father has never been much of a talker about anything. I'm just hoping that there might be a way — if you felt comfortable doing so — for you to talk to the boys about this. Of course, I wouldn't want Stewart to know that I talked to you about it. I just think it would be helpful to him — and to Jack — to feel supported by you. As I said, I know how much they adore you and look up to you, and a kind word at the right moment could really give them the courage to ignore those nasty slurs."

What could I say? I had that feeling that only comes when a teacher is talking to a worried mother with a sincere request for help with a child. I wanted to tell her that I'd help and that everything would be all right. I wanted to tell her that her child was fine, that he was strong and brave, and that a little name calling wouldn't hurt this boy. I sipped my coffee.

"Well, Mrs. Sabinsky —" I began.

"Linda," she said, "Call me Linda. We're both adults."

"Well, Linda," I continued. "There's not a lot that I can do. I think you should know that Stewart is a strong boy. The name-calling might affect him for a while, but ultimately he'll be able to see it for what it is and find the strength to resist changing his friendship because of a couple of jealous boys.

"You don't want me to tell him that we've talked, so I can't very well go up to him and start talking about this. Kids at this age are smarter than that, and I've never been very good at lying. Also — as teachers at Shawmut Hills, we're hired to teach, not to delve into the personal lives of our students." I realized I was quoting Miss Clarkson's line directly. "However, I can promise you this. If I see any of that name calling or get the slightest ink-ling that this is going on in school, I'll deal with it right away and find a way to talk with your son then."

"I hope you won't be too harsh with the other boys," she said, protectively. "I think it's probably very typical of kids this age these days."

"It is," I continued, "but I think it's the responsibility of the teacher to deal with this kind of thing swiftly and firmly. It really does have the potential for making all the kids distant from their friends and, as I remember from my own school days, sixth grade is a very special time for those friendships."

"It was the same way for me," Linda said with a smile as she let her mind wander back 25 years. "I was best friends with little Allison Barclay — who later became Miss South Carolina — and we wore the same clothes to school and arranged our hair alike and just spent all of our time together."

"I promise to handle this the best way I can," I said. I left a dollar for our check, took up my backpack and said goodbye, then dashed out the door to catch the bus into town.

The opportunity to talk with the boys came up sooner than I had imagined. The following day at school, as my students were en-gaged in a variety of small-group projects for our Middle Ages class, I was distracted from work at my desk by a commotion at the rear of the room. Stewart and Jack — who were building a sugar-cube model of a medieval castle — were arguing with two other boys who wanted to use the container of paste. Before I could intervene, nasty words were flying, the paste can went sailing through the air, and a chorus of "Gay! Gay! Gay!" taunts was mounting. Jack, the biggest boy in class, was turning beet red. As he lost his temper and started swinging in all directions, teacher arrived on the scene.

I pulled the four boys directly involved in the incident into the conference room adjacent to the classroom and closed the door. I immediately confronted the troublemakers.

"Arthur and Scott, just what is going on here?" I insisted on knowing.

"They wouldn't let us use the paste," Arthur whined, shaking his head of curly hair, as if this explanation might be suitable for anything short of nuclear war.

"We would too!" Stewart insisted, the words spitting out from between his teeth. "But you've been calling us names all week and now you expect us to let you use the paste? Good luck brother."

I thought it would help to clarify the issues at stake here. "There are two things going on here that I can see," I began. "One involves who gets to use the paste — which is the property of this school — and the other involves name calling. Let's talk about the paste first."

After a five minute discussion, during which each boy vented his feelings about use of the paste, who needed the paste more immediately, and if there would be enough paste for everyone to get their projects finished, we turned to the second issue.

"I want it to be very clear," I said looking directly at Scott and Arthur, "that name calling like what went on here today is not at all acceptable in this classroom. If you have a problem with someone, you're going to have to find another way to resolve it. Furthermore, the use of the word 'gay' in a nasty way won't be tolerated as well. Just like we don't allow racial and ethnic slurs, we will not allow any kind of prejudice in this classroom."

It took a bit of a threat to extract a commitment from the

boys to curtail name-calling — specifically the information that their parents would be notified if such taunting occurred again. With the promises stated, and the intensity talked out of the situation, I sent Scott and Arthur back to their shield building. Then I turned to Stewart and Jack.

"I know how difficult it can be for a couple of guys to be good friends, especially when the other boys in the class become jealous and nasty about it. I want you to know that I won't tolerate any of that name calling and I hope you will let me know if other incidents arise."

"I'm not sure I'm going to tattle on the other kids," said Jack, falling right into his role as the big man of the classroom.

"I don't really expect you to do that," I added. "But I do want you to know that when people get jealous, they do all kinds of nasty things and that you can get help and support from teacher if you want to."

Stewart shifted the focus of the discussion a bit. "It's not that I mind the name-calling, so much," he began, in his reasonable, calculated manner. "I don't care what they call us. If Jack and I want to do a lot of things together, that's our business and everyone else should keep out. We both have girlfriends, you know, so it's all okay. I don't care what anyone says, Jack's my best friend."

Jack himself wasn't as calm. "It just gets me so angry when the guys do that. I just wish they'd leave us alone. It's just that they all want to be our friends and are jealous because we spend so much time together. Arthur's angry because he invited me over to his house last weekend and I was going to the football game at Harvard with Stewart."

"Maybe it would have been better for you to have gone over to Arthur's house," Stewart added.

"I think it's important for you to make your own decisions about who you spend time with and not let your classmates pressure you. Friendship is a very important thing and it's just too bad that some people become jealous and start to do hurtful things. I hope you don't let it damage your friendship."

An awkward moment of silence lapsed and then Stewart

looked up. "Can we go now, Mr. Rofes?" he asked in an innocent voice.

"I think it's time we all went back to work," I said, holding the door to the classroom open for both of them. The two little men escaped back into the classroom and again entered their sugarcube medieval fantasies.

3

As we returned from Thanksgiving break and I realized that the initial excitement of my new work situation had died away, my feelings of isolation at the school increased. By December, I felt generally confident, capable, and well-received by faculty members, parents and students alike. I was somehow managing to keep on top of my classroom duties, and beginning to get involved in the working committees of the school which were involved — in small ways — with curricular policy and decisionmaking.

I had devoted most of my out-of-school time during the fall to either lesson preparation or deep slumber. But as winter approached and I gained a greater reserve of energy, I found myself wanting to become more active in organizations within the gay community. At the age of twenty-two, I was coming to the end of a five-year struggle to accept my homosexuality. As a kid, I had engaged in much of the same-sex fooling around that appears to be common among American boys. Cub Scout activities, and later Boy Scout camp, initiated me into these rites, in a context that made it apparent that most — if not *all* — boys enjoyed playing in one another's trousers. It wasn't until I was 13 — at a Jewish Federation Camp for boys and girls in the Catskills of New

York — that I realized that my attraction to other boys was no longer socially acceptable. Camp Wel-Met provided me with a few summers of participation in young adolescent heterosexual mating rituals and finally, as a staffer at the age of seventeen, the first clumsy passion of my life.

As an assistant to the camp director, I was responsible for many mundane tasks that proved challenging to me. I learned to drive the camp's temperamental pick-up truck, to check in and distribute camp supplies to cabins throughout the camp, and to make nightly rounds on foot at eleven o'clock to every unit of cabins, during which I would exchange words with the counselor-on-duty, collect daily reports, and bid them goodnight. It was during one of these late night rounds that I found myself receiving reports from a golden-haired boy with deep hazel eyes that twinkled in delight as he recounted the raids that had ensued during the previous two hours by the nine-year-olds in his charge. Short, handsome, and with early summer freckles dotting his nose, Josh Berger flashed like summer lightning into my life, and this insecure, awkward beanpole would never be the same.

July and August were filled with the antics of two boys who found friendship and adventure along the Delaware River. Shared excursions took us canoeing through the river's rapids, hitch-hiking to delicatessens in Monticello, the nearest town, and camping on spits of land extending into that blue-white water. We'd arrange to take our weekly free day together and leave secret messages in undecipherable codes under each other's pillow. It was a summer to read Kerouac novels, sing Joni Mitchell songs and hate Richard Nixon. To me, it was — at the same time — one last fling at boyhood and one terrifying entrance into adult reality.

Josh and I never discussed the sex. I can't recall if we knew the words, but our mouths certainly could not emit that vocabulary. At times today, I find it difficult to believe that it all actually happened. Like so many boys before us and after us, we used the excuse of alcohol to cover our tracks. Coming back to my room in the staff lodge late at night after an evening at the bar adjacent to campgrounds, we'd give one another a massage and fumble with each other's genitals. We knew it felt good and we knew we wanted each other. Beyond that, we could not admit, to one another or to ourselves, the significance of that summer.

My love affair with Josh lasted a twisted two years — fighting his fear and denial and rejection all the way. After I arrived in Cambridge during the fall to begin my freshman year at college, we spoke often and I visited Josh frequently, sometimes hitch-hiking eight hours to visit him at the State University of New York at Binghamton. I found the courage to make weekly forays into Boston and discovered gay bars and the men who frequent them. I kissed my first man that fall — I understand now how Josh's refusal to kiss me was a function of his emotional denial of our actions — and learned the words for naming who and what I was.

The pain that came with the limitations Josh set on our friendship was with me throughout my four years at college, as was the pain that came with my pulling away from my high school girlfriend, in an attempt to be honest with myself. Harvard was as much for me an institution that thrust me into the world of Shakespeare and Pascal, as a setting for me to work through the complex crises of an identity in formation. Looking back at my younger self, the signs had always been there. Somehow, through a crazy four years of academic competition and social mani-pulation, Harvard managed to spit me back out into the world, sure of myself, my needs and my desires.

During the summer of 1976, amid the fanfare of graduation, the Bicentennial celebration in Boston, and my uncertainty about the future, I created a life for myself. I found myself a home with five new friends in a big old house in working-class Somerville, a ten-minute bus ride from Harvard Square. Through these people, I entered the world of progressive politics — a bit on the wane, even in Boston, since the heyday of the 60's and early 70's. My housemates were all politically aware people, holding daytime jobs or going to school, and working evenings and weekends on a range of political issues: one woman at the Women's Health Pro-ject and a foundation that funded radical organizations; another at a progressive science and technology journal; one man at a teen center for Somerville youth; while another male roommate was active in men's consciousness-raising groups. Holly, my closest friend in the house, worked at a project supporting the desegregation of the Boston schools.

I was different. I was the only gay person in the house, the only recent college graduate, and the only novice in the world of radical politics. But learn I did that fall, under the constant tutelage of the Putnam Street house. With their full knowledge and support, I became involved in Boston's fledgling gay movement and began volunteer work at the *Gay Community News*, a three-year-old weekly publication. I became involved in Boston's Gay Men's Center, an attempt by local men to create an alternative meeting center for socializing, community education and political work. Since I no longer drank, and since I was still intimidated by the "scene" that accompanied much of gay urban culture, I was excited about the development of such a center, and attended several of the planning meetings to help hash out the working details of the center. I quickly became involved in a whirl of activities and, simultaneously, a new network of men. I became involved in several short romances related to my work at the center — one with a very kind man who enjoyed sitting in front of the television on Saturday nights and making out like teenagers, and one with a very confused man who seemed most to enjoy manipulating me through weeks of flirtation.

My new life only increased my sense of isolation at the school. During off-school hours, I found myself surrounded by politically aware men and women, many of whom were gay and believed that it was important for an individual to make an open statement about being gay. Originally I resented this attempt to meld politics to people's personal lives. But after a few months of activity at the center and the newspaper offices, I found myself beginning to feel more open to the political aspects of being homosexual. While being gay initially seemed a profoundly personal experience to me, I saw decent, hard-working people lose their jobs simply because of their homosexuality. One lesbian friend of our household was denied visitation rights with her children, simply because she was a lesbian. It became impossible to deny that my sexuality was political. As my housemate working on women's health issues told me, "Honey," she said, "there ain't nothing that goes on below the waist that isn't political these days. And a lot, also, that's above the waist!"

The growth and development of my gay identity began to effect my feeling about teaching at Shawmut Hills. I felt isolated, alone, and perhaps what is worse, slightly hypocritical for maintaining my cover. I was able to rationalize what I was doing, but my rationalization was not able to go unchallenged for very long. And having no one at school with whom to talk about the compromises and deceptions was the most difficult part of the experience. Yet I still felt the daily fear of being "caught" and yanked from my closet.

One day, a small dance and mime troupe performed at our weekly all-school assembly. The group of two men and two women performed modern dance and mime technique that amused the younger children, but made my own pre-adolescents very uncomfortable. The drama and art teacher was in charge of scheduling performers in the school. During one act of this troupe, the two men had their arms around each other. Ordinarily this would have been fine, but here the men were dressed in body stockings and ballet slippers, and when one of them wore an earring and spoke with a lisp, awkward giggles came out of my kids. I also noticed Chuck Ritter, the boys' gym teacher, looking very uncomfortable and checking the clock on the wall to see how much time remained in the performance.

After the assembly ended, it was time for mid-morning break. The children put on their coats and ran outside into the December chill for fifteen minutes of fun and games while the teachers retreated to the faculty room. I found myself having coffee with a group that included Alice and Marie, the French teacher.

"Quite a performance today, eh?" began Marie in her pert French accent.

"I thought Beatrice was going to drop dead right then and there when those two guys put their arms around each other in that skit," said Alice with a laugh. "And that she managed to keep her composure — and even gave that same thank you speech she always makes after a performance — was really quite remarkable. I watched her throughout the performance and really thought she was going to die."

"Your kids got a few chuckles in, didn't they, Eric?" Marie asked. "I noticed Jack Andrews sitting there, red-faced the entire time, and when that one man began to speak and he lisped . . ."

"I don't know what else we could have expected from sixth graders," Alice said. "They're always right on the edge of giggles when it comes to anything that has to do with sex roles, sexuality, or the boy-girl issues."

Another faculty member chimed in. "I'm a science teacher, and I'll tell you this wasn't boy-girl issues. It was boy-boy issues. I just don't know how our eminent drama teacher Zayna could have allowed this stuff to go on. I've got to teach those boys math in ten minutes, and I know it's going to be an impossible task."

Before anyone could respond the door of the faculty room pushed open and in walked Chuck Ritter with a basketball under his arm. "How'd you all like the show today?" he asked with a sheepish grin on his face. "She'll be bringing in Liberace next week and, after that, we'll have Fags on Parade."

Chuck's joke broke the tension in the room and everyone laughed. The science teacher jumped in, "I think you're being a little harsh, Chuck. I appreciate Zayna's attempt to bring a little culture into this stodgy school. I guess it's not her fault if a dance company turns out to be a bunch of homos."

"Yeah, well Clarkson nearly shit a brick when those two guys started going at it," Chuck continued. "Zayna's down in her office now, and you can bet Clarkson won't let her get away with that again."

Alice and I looked at each other. Neither of us said anything. Finally, I glanced over at Marie, who was, in fact, watching Alice and me look at each other. Marie got up from her seat and headed to the coffee maker for another cup of coffee. "I don't know why we're all freaking out about the show today. A little bit of culture isn't going to hurt the kids. Clarkson is so uptight that she'd get upset if any two people were touching each other in front of the kids — boys with boys *or* boys with girls. And, Chucky, words like 'fags' and 'homos' aren't used much anymore. My husband has several friends who are . . . that way . . . and they seem to prefer to be called 'gay.'"

Chuck looked back at her, just a little bit embarrassed. Then the science teacher responded.

"I suppose you're right, Marie," she said. "But these kids come from pretty conservative homes, and I doubt the parents would approve of this. And, after all, this is a private school and we're here to do what the parents want. That's why they pay to send their kids here."

"Incorrect," Marie said adamantly. "We're here to do what we think is best for the kids and if their parents don't like it, they should take their kids and their money elsewhere."

"Before this debate escalates," Alice said, looking at her watch, "we'd better head back to the classrooms. Break ends in about thirty seconds and I've got 45 second-graders coming into the library to watch 'Spiders of South America.'"

Five teachers quickly dropped their coffee cups on the cart and moved out of the faculty room to the classrooms. One teacher had said nothing at all during the preceding discussion.

Parental desires and expectations were a major preoccupation of teachers at the school, and for good reason — in private schools there is a precarious and unspoken peace maintained between parent and teacher. It is unclear, for example, whether teachers are hired based on their teaching skills and program development experience or whether they are hired simply to satisfy the day-to-day wishes of the children's parents. Hence, at the root of the relationship lies a great deal of ambiguity.

The school's annual Parent-Teacher Dinner was held in late December. It was made clear to all teachers that we were expected to show up and greet any parents that we had yet to meet and parents — particularly mothers — were expected to try to outdo one another in a suburban gourmet potluck supper. I was informed that sports coats and ties were the appropriate attire for the occasion, and the invitation from the school board requested that teachers "invite" their spouses to the occasion — I suppose an attempt to impress on the parents that their wholesome, family values were shared by the faculty. I dreaded the event, but, as Alice told me, this kind of function "comes with the job."

I arrived at the school that Saturday evening with my "date," Ellen, a friend from college who was a pleasant person to be with at this kind of social occasion. Always able to make charming conversation with strangers, I felt that Ellen would smooth things over between awkward me and the rest of the world. Ellen was also — in my eye — beautiful and I admitted to myself that one reason I often asked her to be my cover was to provide the public with the impression that I was able to attract intelligent, beautiful women.

As we walked in we were greeted by Miss Clarkson, staffing the reception table, ready with specially lettered name-tags for all the teachers.

"Good evening, Eric," she said in her normal, professional voice, tinged with but a hint of social warmth.

"Good evening, Miss Clarkson," I responded. "I'd like you to meet my friend, Ellen Kaplan."

As the two exchanged greetings, the pit of my stomach began to feel all those wonderful feelings that frequently accompany mendacity. I knew Clarkson was sizing this woman up as my girl-friend and I knew that Ellen knew that this was going on and that she was my cover for the evening. It was an outrageously con-trived situation, and neither Ellen nor I were comfortable. I envi-sioned Clarkson assuming Ellen to be my soon-to-be fiancée and realized that the assumption of heterosexuality was so strong, especially in communities like Shawmut Hills, that it would be easy for everyone to expect Ellen and me to be wed shortly follow-ing the potluck. My stomach tightened and coiled in a knot.

As we walked into the school's dining hall, where the tables were slowly being filled with quiches, casseroles, chicken wings, hams and turkeys, Marie approached.

"Bonjour, Eric. I'd like you to meet my husband, Ron," she said in a cheery voice. "And I haven't met your friend yet."

I managed to fulfill the expectant social role, despite my stomach. "Marie and Ron, this is my friend Ellen."

"Eric teaches the sixth grade class at Shawmut," Marie told her husband, "and, just between us, he and I are the only teachers in this school with any sense of fun."

"What class do you teach?" Ellen asked.

I jumped in. "Marie teaches French. We're both in our first year at the school, and I think we're both feeling our way blindly through the year."

Marie continued. "I'm not feeling my way blindly anywhere tonight. I left Ron for a moment to go to the little girls' room, and was accosted by the father of a fourth grade student, who seemed to want to feel his way blindly with me," she joked. "I'm planning on charging sexual harrassment at next Tuesday's faculty meeting."

If anyone was going to have this kind of problem, it was not surprising that it would be Marie. Her shoulder-length reddish-brown hair, beautiful green eyes, and perfect skin made her one of the few teachers with a sense of style. Marie always wore attractive fashions that set off her figure and — I was sure — she would need to be prepared for passes from horny suburban men all evening. Her French background and accent gave her more than a touch of the exotic.

"Whose father was this?" I asked.

"Little Jimmy Ryan's dad — you know, the cute little rolly-polly boy with the funny nasal voice," she answered. "I should have seen this coming, since he's already set up two conferences with me and, at each one, seemed more interested in talking about what he terms 'my background' than his son's French problems. And his wife is an absolute doll. I don't know what he's trying to do with me." She put her arm around Ron's waist. "Thank goodness my big strong husband is here to protect me tonight."

The conversation was broken up by the arrival of Chuck Ritter, accompanied by a woman in what appeared to be a full-length evening gown. "Eric, Marie, I'd like you to meet my girlfriend, Mary Jo," he said. "She teaches gym at Lexington Girls' Academy."

After quick introductions, Chuck noticed the tables of food throughout the dining hall. "When do we start eating?" he asked.

Food was something Chuck and I could talk about with one mind. "It looks as if Clarkson's about to start the food line rolling," I said, looking over towards the headmistress who, along with a busy bunch of mothers, was starting to remove foil coverings from the dishes.

Immediately, with neither announcement nor formal signal, the crowd surged toward the tables. Surprisingly, I found myself and Chuck at the front of the line, filling plates for ourselves and our "girlfriends."

"Eager boys, aren't you?" I heard from one of the servers behind the table. I looked up to see Linda Sabinsky smiling at me. "Here, try some of these," she said, spooning little marinated chunks of beef onto my plate. "Annette Green makes these each year, and they are really super. And, by the way, I like the looks of your friend. Please be sure you introduce her to me, once you cowboys are finished going through the chow line."

With my plate laden down with a little bit of every dish on the tables (I wouldn't want to risk offending any of my kids' parents who had worked so hard to prepare a dish for the evening), I stepped into the adjacent gymnasium, which was decorated and set for the party this evening. Ellen was seated on the far side of the room, at a table with Marie, and she was waving me over. After stumbling through the crowds, I managed to navigate myself to our table without spilling the food off the weak little paper plates that always make potlucks like this a real challenge for pigs like me.

Seated next to Ellen, with Chuck and his date, as well as Marie and her husband at the table, I finally had a moment to relax and survey the crowd. The parent body of the school was well-dressed in conservative suits and dresses. I was sure the parents of several of my students were looking toward me, sizing up my relationship with Ellen, and trying to catch my eye. I nodded or waved hello to them, and continued gazing around the room. I was beginning to feel at ease at the dinner.

The women were generally an attractive bunch, with their hair done specifically for the occasion and their make-up perfect. They seemed spirited, at ease, and happy to be at a dinner at their childrens' school. The men were a more diverse group. Some looked bored and put upon by having to spend this evening socializing. A few men in the far corner of the room were discussing some subject loudly and making large, sweeping gestures with their hands and fingers. I imagined them discussing football or politics.

There were, however, a few very attractive men in the room; now that I had a second to sit and breathe, my eyes fell on them. Cruising straight men was not a favorite pastime of mine, but I did notice the thin, bearded man at the next table who had a warm smile and kept getting up to refill his wife's wine glass. The husband of one of the kindergarten teachers looked awfully bored as he was introduced to one parent after another, but his curly blond hair and blue eyes must have endeared him to everyone. As I glanced around the room, surveying the attractive men at various tables, my eyes unconsciously settled upon one man in particular.

As recognition dawned on me, I said aloud, "Oh my god." Fortunately, the rest of my table was engaged in conversation and only Ellen heard me and noted my startled look.

"What's the matter?" she asked.

I squinted my eyes a bit so I could be sure of what I saw. There, at a table halfway across the room, was a man I could swear I'd seen frequently at Sporters, one of my favorite gay bars on Beacon Hill. Short, bearded, and stocky with muscle, he had always seemed to be one of the friendlier people at the bar and, while I had never talked to him myself, he was one of those guys who seemed to know everyone in the place. I had spent many an evening watching him greet one man after another, buying beers for his friends, talking and joking. My stomach again twisted tightly.

"I'm not really sure," I said quietly to Ellen, "but over there is a man I swear I recognize from Sporters."

"What, may I ask, is Sporters?" Ellen asked.

"A bar on Beacon Hill for people like me." And then I said quickly, "I hope he doesn't recognize me."

"Are you sure it's the same guy?" Ellen asked.

I hesitated a moment. "I think so. I've always thought that he was kind of cute, and he's very popular at the bar. I've watched him talk with a lot of people."

"Are you nervous about his possibly recognizing you?" she asked.

"Of course I am. I'm not prepared for this at all. What's he doing here? Who does he think he is?" I asked, speaking without thinking.

"I suppose he's the father of one of the kids in the school, or else he's here as the 'date' of one of the mothers," Ellen answered with a smirk on her face. "Like someone else I know."

"I just know I won't be able to deal with it if he recognizes me," I said, thinking out loud. "I just can't deal with this kind of pressure on me tonight."

Just as I began to get nervous about being spotted by this man, I felt a tap on my shoulder. Turning around, I was face to face with Annette Green.

"Eric, there are so many parents here of the children in your class who are absolutely dying to meet you," she said in her saccharine, high-pitched voice. "I don't suppose you could leave your table for a few minutes and make the rounds with me? After all, this is supposed to be a dinner where the parents and teachers meet — rather than isolating the teachers with the teachers and the parents with the parents. Everyone's so excited about the Christmas Play next week, and the stage version of *Beowulf* you've written." Then, noticing Ellen, she turned to her. "I suppose you're Eric's special friend. Hello. My name is Annette Green, I don't believe we've been introduced."

I jumped in and introduced them. Annette's eyes took in Ellen and I knew she was assessing her and developing a full scenario for our relationship.

I allowed Annette to lead me through the crowds and introduce me to some of the parents in the class. Many of them I'd managed to meet during the early days of school. While I had met many of the mothers, the fathers were mostly new to me. Since I had practiced my handshake ("Firm enough?" I'd asked Paul last week as we practiced what we called the school teacher's handshake — firm and quick), I confidently met the men and answered their questions. It seemed to be routine to question where I'd gone to college, and my Ivy League response always prompted a question about Harvard football. Summoning all the social skills I had developed during my four years amid the sons of ambassadors and public officials, I ducked the question and moved the conversation forward. After about a dozen exchanges, and as many struggles to avoid lapsing into long conversation about Johnny's spelling skills, I found myself returning to the dining room to check out the desserts.

Linda Sabinsky still stood behind the dessert table, directing all comers to the special treats. "I want to thank you for how you handled the situation with Stewart and Jack a few weeks ago," she said. "Stewart told me what happened and said that you were very helpful and supportive. His father and I really do appreciate your help with the matter."

"All in the line of duty," I said jokingly, beginning to feel like a character on a television sitcom who was speaking dialogue written by a vapid Hollywood writer. I helped myself to brownies, and cheesecake, and a little ice cream, and fresh fruit. As my plate slowly became filled with sweet things, I realized that the ice cream was starting to run into the cheesecake, and I tried to remedy the situation by returning to my seat. As I quickly swerved around to head for the door into the gymnasium, my ample plate of goodies smacked directly into the man behind me.

I looked up directly from the plate, to the mess on the shirt, to the man's face and there, smiling at me, was the man I'd recognized from Sporters.

I was stunned. "Oh, I'm awfully sorry," I apologized, looking at the coffee ice cream and fruit pie staining his white shirt and striped tie.

"It's my fault," he insisted graciously. "I wasn't watching where I was going in my rush to get some of those desserts."

"Let me help clean some of that mess off," I said, putting my plate down on the nearest counter.

Linda Sabinsky was already on the scene with a sponge and paper towel. "I'm not sure if you two have met," she said, wiping away at the ice cream stain. "This is Stewart's new teacher, Eric Rofes," she said to Mr. Sporters, "and this in my good friend Michael Reich whose son Timmy is in the fourth grade. Michael is also the chairman of our Parent Committee."

We shook hands and I again apologized for the mess on his shirt.

"Oh don't apologize to Michael," Linda insisted. "This happens at every dinner party he goes to, and every school potluck. It wouldn't be a party if Michael Reich didn't end up with food stains."

He smiled a beautiful smile which spread ear-to-ear. "Now, Linda, there's no reason to exaggerate," he said good naturedly. "And I want to be sure that our new teachers don't think of the Parent Committee as a bunch of slobs who can't keep ice cream off their shirts."

Linda finished wiping the shirt. "That's the best I'm going to be able to do tonight. Take the shirt home and have Adele soak it in bleach. I'm sure it'll be all right. Now, I've got to return to my post behind the fudge sauce."

I was left awkwardly standing with Mr. Reich, hoping he hadn't recognized me, and wondering if I were possibly mistaken about this man. "So you're the new sixth grade teacher," he said. "Where'd you used to teach?"

I'd already answered the question about a dozen times this

evening. "I've just graduated from college and, except for student teaching, this is my first job."

The next question was predictable. "Where did you go to college?" he asked.

"I graduated from Harvard last spring," I answered. "And I studied education and English."

"Oh yeah?" he said. "Did you play basketball there?"

"No I didn't," I said, sick of the sports questions thrown my way all evening.

"I'm only asking because you look familiar to me," he said. "I teach there in the biology labs, but I don't have a lot of contact with the undergraduates. A buddy of mine coaches the basketball team, so I go to some of the games, and I thought I might have seen you there."

Feeling like this man was striking a bit too close to home, I decided to hasten the conversation. "No, not me. I played a little intramural basketball," I lied, "but not on the varsity or the j.v. teams."

"Still, you look familiar," he insisted on pursuing the matter. "Did you study biology or work in the labs at all?"

"No, I didn't."

"Well, I'm probably mistaken then," he said, looking down at my plate of desserts, currently becoming soup. "Looks as if you ought to head back to your table before there's nothing left of your dessert but mush. It's been a pleasure to meet you, and I'm sure I'll see you throughout the year.

I said goodbye, gave a final apology for the crash into his shirt, and hurriedly retreated back to Ellen.

After returning to the table, I told Ellen what had happened. She was amused by the story, and had a difficult time understanding my fears and nervousness surrounding this unfortunate way of meeting Mr. Sporters. "Maybe he really didn't recognize you," she argued. "You and I know how good looking you are, but perhaps this man has other tastes and never noticed you in the bar."

"I just don't like the idea of having a parent in the school —

the head of the Parent Committee, no less — running around in my bars — even if he is . . . " I hesitated to say the word, as if the gymnasium wall we sat near had ears and the word would echo throughout the room.

"You're just nervous about him blowing your cover," she said quietly. "Not to change the subject — but why are all our desserts in a bowl of soupy ice cream? I can't eat this mess!"

With that, Ellen got up and went to replace her bowl of desserts and I recovered from the incident by spooning soupy cheesecake into my mouth.

The rest of the dinner went smoothly, filled with presentations by Miss Clarkson, as well as the president of the school board, and by Alice, the head of the Faculty Council. Teachers were at an unfair disadvantage throughout the evening, as it was easy for parents to remember their child's teacher, but not very easy for a solitary teacher to recall 25 sets of parents. Still, most of the socializing took place amongst peers — parent-to-parent or teacher-to-teacher — which made things more comfortable for both parties.

Afterward, driving home after dropping Ellen in Cambridge, I tried to understand why I was so disturbed about discovering a gay father in the school. What could he do to me? Expose me? If he was hanging around Sporters, he had as much to hide as I did — especially if he was still married.

I finally realized what was occurring.

After a few months at Shawmut Hills, I had adjusted to leading a schizoid life. I had my "teacher Eric" and my "gay Eric" and the two were kept fully separated. When I was at school, or at a school function, I was strictly a professional teacher. When I was outside of school, on my own time evenings and weekends, I was a different person, growing into active involvement in progressive politics and the gay community. Just as I refused to reveal the "gay Eric" to people within school, I was reluctant to discuss my professional life outside Shawmut Hills. I once refused to name the place where I worked when asked one evening by a teacher I'd met at the Gay Men's Center. Meeting Michael Reich upset the balance I had worked hard to achieve. The thought of mixing the two worlds — or even one world knowing that the other world was out there — threatened the precarious foundation of my life.

When I returned home, my housemate Holly was still awake, sitting in the kitchen drinking tea and putting the finishing touches on a new brochure about desegregation and Boston high schools. Holly taught in the Boston Public Schools, and we frequently discussed educational issues. A few years older than me, she had taught in Boston for several years and was deeply involved in the controversies surrounding busing.

"It was strange, Holly," I said as I poured myself some tea. "There was this man there — the father of one of the kids in the school and a member of the Parent Committee — who I recognized from a gay bar. It made me feel very uncomfortable."

"I was waiting for this to happen, Eric," she said, looking at me a bit perplexed. Holly had many gay friends and seemed to understand the problems gay people faced.

"For what to happen?"

"For your double life to catch up with you."

"This is no time to play Agatha Christie."

"I'm serious. Even if you want to keep your teaching job separate from your politics and your social life, you're going to find it very difficult. I'm surprised you haven't seen more people at your school you recognize from bars and parties."

"Most gay teachers seem to do it, don't they?"

"You know, where I work, a lot of the teachers are gay. Some are sort of open about it and some aren't."

"Yeah, I remember your friend Angie that came to dinner here a few months ago."

"She's an example of one of those who tries to keep it secret and she can't. I team-taught with her two years ago and she's never told me she's a lesbian, but I know she is."

"Have you ever tried to bring up the subject?" I asked.

"Sure. I told her once that I live with a gay guy, hoping she'd feel comfortable enough to come out to me, but she didn't then and she hasn't yet."

I thought to myself a bit and then I asked Holly, "Would you say that a lot of school teachers are gay?"

"That's a strange question, coming from you, Mr. Gay Activist."

"What do you mean?"

"Sure there are a lot. If you look back over the years, I think most of those women who we had as teachers — those spinster schoolmarms — were really closeted lesbians. You've taken survey courses on American education, haven't you? Until the middle of this century, it wasn't acceptable for a teacher to be married, and certainly unacceptable for a woman teacher to be pregnant. So a lot of the teachers who worked with kids must have been gay."

"In fact," she continued, "I read an article in one of those gay magazines that you leave around the house, that talked about all the famous teachers throughout history — everyone from Socrates and Plato, down through M. Carey Thomas, F.O. Matthiessen, and that woman who ran Shadyside School all those years. Even the mythical teachers in literature — Jean Brody, Ichabod Crane, Wing Biddlebaum — are suspect. Sure, gay teachers are all over the place. It's being open about it that seems difficult.

"Let me tell you one more thing, before I go up to bed," Holly said finally. "As a straight woman trying her best to meet a nice guy at work, I can testify to one thing. Most of the attractive, friendly men who aren't chauvinists and aren't married, turn out to be gay."

— 4 —

"Take out a sheet of looseleaf paper and begin by writing your name, in script, on the top line at the left margin and today's date, January 23, 1977, on the top right. Skip two lines and then write the title of this composition in the center of the line. The title is "One Important Person." Be sure to underline the title. Now let me tell you what this paper is about.

"Your assignment is to choose one person who has done a tremendous amount of good for the world, or one person who has done a tremendous amount of harm for the world, and write about that person, being sure to explain why you feel he or she has been so important. You may choose any person as long as the person is still alive today."

Groans from the class. A few hands shot up.

"Mr. Rofes, does it have to be just one person?" asked Ann, who seemed to cultivate the revolting habit of squeezing her face into a quizzical expression that bore an uncanny resemblance to a gargoyle with pigtails.

"Who can answer Ann's question?" I asked the group. "Stewart, what's the answer?"

"You said that we should choose one person — not more than one," he responded.

63

"Thank you, Stewart. Are there any other questions?"

"I have one," Arthur squeaked. "How long does the composition have to be?"

"That's a good question, Arthur," I admitted. "I omitted that information, didn't I? The composition, which is due at the end of this class, should be at least one page long. Please write in script and in ink, and be sure to correct your spelling and proofread for grammatical errors."

Ann raised her hand again. "Does the person have to be alive? I mean, can it be a person who did a lot of good back in the Middle Ages? Or can it be a person like George Washington?" Her face was again melodramatically squinched up, which made her questions seem even more inappropriate to the other children. Since the others were already laughing at her, and since it appeared Ann must have been playing with her pigtails or otherwise distracted during my announcement of the assignment, I answered the question myself.

"The person must be alive today, Ann. Now we have no more time for questions. I'd like you all to get started. If anyone has an important question, or is having difficulty beginning their work, please come up to my desk. Otherwise, I'll notify you when a half hour remains. Get to work."

The room became silent as the children began their compositions. Some sat, staring out the window, wondering who they should choose for the theme. Others began in haste, writing quickly and with animation and enthusiasm. Still others had the difficult problem of beginning the composition several times, changing their minds, squeezing pieces of paper into tight balls, and beginning again.

Meanwhile, I sat at the desk, grading history tests from a handy answer key I had devised the night before. The children hated tests — or so they professed — but the only thing they seemed to hate more was a long delay in my grading their exams. It was a treat for them to receive tests back quickly and since I enjoyed showing that I'd work hard to please them — and since it meant no papers to lurk over me for days on end — I often tried to

return exams at the end of the day. This kept me efficient, un-
burdened, and somewhat popular with my students.

Throughout the hour, most of the children worked with care
and concentration on their papers. Ann managed to come up and
whine a bit, asking more questions and complaining that the
assignment was too specific. Several students asked for permission to visit the library to look up some information about
their chosen famous person. By the time I gave them the "five
minute warning," most of the students were finished with their
compositions and beginning to exchange papers and read each
other's works.

At two o'clock, I told the students to put down their pens and
their papers and asked for volunteers to read papers out loud to
the class. The usual half-dozen hands were raised, and we heard
eleven-year-old viewpoints on why Jimmy Carter was a force for
good in the world (peace in the Middle East), and why the singer
Cher was a force for evil (her music was boring and had dumb
lyrics). I heard why Mohammed Ali was the greatest athlete and
pundit who ever lived, and why tennis player Jimmy Connors
was a jerk. Finally, one of my more thoughtful students,
Deborah, a quiet, mature girl who was tall for her age, raised her
hand and began to read her paper.

"My paper is about Anita Bryant," Deborah said in her
poised, understated voice. She began reading. "Many people
know Anita Bryant as the orange juice lady. She is on television
selling Florida orange juice all the time. Sometimes she brings her
whole family with her, and she is shown pouring them juice for
breakfast from the Florida sunshine tree.

"Lately, Anita Bryant has become famous because she is
working against gays. She doesn't think that gay people should
have any rights, and she has been getting into the newspapers and
on television for this opinion. She has become a controversial
person and not just an orange juice lady.

"I think she has done a lot of good for the world, because it is
important for people to speak their mind and bring up topics like
this. Some people think that gay people should be schoolteachers

or doctors or other jobs, but Anita Bryant thinks they shouldn't. She also thinks it's bad for children to have to be around these kinds of people. Her idea is called 'Save the Children' and she is doing this because she cares about children. It is important for adults to stick up for children, because we don't have a lot of say in the government and we can't vote."

Deborah took her seat. As always, after a child had read an original work, I asked the others to give feedback — criticism both positive and negative. Several hands went up immediately.

"I agree with you," Scott said. This was one of those rare occasions on which he didn't seem to be joking. "I thought of doing my paper on her, but I didn't know enough about her to fill up a whole piece of paper and I like Mohammed Ali better."

Ann waved her hand frantically. "I wrote mine on Anita Bryant, too, and I took the other side. Let me read my paper now."

I assented and Ann read her paper. She seemed fairly well-informed about the happenings taking place at this time in Florida and she expressed strong concern that nasty things were being done to innocent — albeit, weird — people. Her paper ended, "I think that someday, people are going to realize that two people in this century did the worst kinds of work against other people. One was Adolph Hitler and the other was Anita Bryant."

From the conversations whispering around the room and from the hands in the air, I realized that this could easily turn into a debate about Anita Bryant. In addition to this not being my priority for the day — I wanted to have these papers read and turned in to me — I was uncomfortable dealing again with this topic so directly. I looked for a way to diffuse the energy that was peaking in the classroom.

"I know that many of you would like to talk about Anita Bryant, but that's not what we're going to do today," I said. "Maybe at another time, if someone wanted to bring in an article from the newspaper, we could discuss this topic in current events. For now, I'd like to shift the focus of the discussion a little, and see if there is any other situation where someone wrote that a

specific person was a good person for the world and someone else
wrote that the person was not?"

We compared information and the names of people who had
been written about. It seems that the major villian of these
children was Richard Nixon, and the major heroes were their
mothers, but there was no other situation where the same individual fell on both sides. As we finished this comparison, the bell
rang; I hurriedly collected the papers, announced homework
assignments, and passed back the history tests. The kids were out
the door by 3:05 and I sat there, looking at 25 compositions which
I would spend the night reading, correcting, and commenting
upon. A teacher's work — as any teacher can (and will) tell you —
is never done.

Later that evening, as I sat at my desk grading the papers, Holly
knocked on the door and came in. She picked up a handful of the
compositions and scanned them with her eagle eye.

"This is some collection of writings, huh, Eric?" she said.
"My high school students would have chosen a whole different
set of heroes and villians. Mohammed Ali would certainly merit
more than one paper — and none of your white suburban kids
wrote about Martin Luther King, did they? You're falling down in
your work, dear," she teased.

"They wrote Martin Luther King stories last week, when our
school did *not* have a day off for his birthday," I explained defensively. "A lot of the kids complained that public schools had the
day off, and so I asked them what they knew about the man. Most
of them didn't know much except that he was black, so we did a
short unit on him and Rosa Parks. I got some pretty good writings
out of them during that unit."

Holly flipped through the papers and took one out. "Here's
one on Anita Bryant," she said. "What kind of stuff have you been
feeding these kids?"

"That paper was totally unsolicited. I'd never raise her name
in class. Anyway, Holly, you can't imagine how awkwardly I
dealt with it. All the kids wanted to do was discuss the orange

juice lady, and all teacher wanted to do was change the topic quickly."

She looked at me with a puzzled expression on her face. "I can't believe Mr. Militant would lose an opportunity to discuss this issue of gay rights with his children. Are you starting to chicken out on hot topics?"

I became defensive until I turned and saw the smile on her face. "Holly," I said. "I just can't deal with the pressures around discussing gay topics in the classroom. I feel guilty enough about not being Mr. Supergay with the kids. I don't need you to help me feel more guilty."

"Listen." Holly put her arm around my shoulder. "No one expects you to be Supergay or Superman or Superteacher. You're doing the right thing. Stick to your instincts, take risks when you want to take risks, and avoid the flak when you need to. If you don't, I'll tell you this right now, you won't last long in teaching. If you haven't yet heard about teacher burnout, you've just cited one of the major causes. Take things at your own rate. Especially dealing with controversy."

During the final week of January, several interesting pieces of information were dropped in my lap. The first was that my contract probably would be renewed for the following year, as the teacher whom I was replacing while on Sabbatical decided not to return to the school. Also *Beowulf*, our Christmas production, was hailed as such a success by parents that even Miss Clarkson sent me a note of praise for my efforts. The third bit of news was a reminder that my students would be taking standardized achievement tests during the first week of April, which would pre-empt my teaching schedule for that entire week. The fourth — and most surprising — piece of information was that I was expected to teach the school's "human development" program to the fifth and sixth grade boys during the end of the winter. Sex education was thus dropped on me without fanfare or discussion. A note in my box, accompanied by a sample syllabus, was the way this information was conveyed.

Immediately upon hearing this news, I stopped by the library to take out all the books I could find on the topic. As I was rifling through the card catalogue, Alice approached from behind and peered over my shoulder.

"You won't find what you're looking for under 'sex'," she said, pushing her glasses up to the bridge of her nose. "Most classifications for school libraries prefer to use euphemisms. Come over here and let me show you the section of the library where those books are kept. You ought to be familiar with it anyway — your boys spend most of their free library time here. You might as well be aware of what they're reading."

Alice guided me over to a corner of the library.

"Although I know you won't believe it," she said, "I did not deliberately put these books on the highest shelf, out of the reach of most young children."

"Sure, Alice," I said sarcastically. "Sure, I believe you."

"This is honestly where they happen to fall in the classification scheme of things."

"You probably get a real kick out of watching some of the younger kids search for the books."

"As a matter of fact, I do enjoy watching your shorter boys push the stool over to that corner and then try to take some of the books down, all the time watching to see whether anyone is noticing."

Alice sorted through the books on the shelf and selected a few. As she handed them to me, one at a time, she gave a brief synopsis of each book, and indicated its strengths and its weaknesses.

"How do you happen to have these books in the library at all?" I asked her. "Sex education materials in open stack libraries could raise the hackles of some very traditional sorts of people."

"It's a miracle that we have these books and the human development program at all. Some parents had to push hard to get it into the school and it aroused quite a storm of protest from some other parents."

"Have the teachers of the class ever gotten into hot water with the parents?"

"Not that I know of, but that's why it's important for you to make sure that you do a good job teaching the class. If there's one piece of advice I have for you, it's to keep in touch with the kids' parents about what's going on every step of the way."

"Why's that?"

"Otherwise," and she now she spoke with a strong tone of caution in her voice, "some parent is going to make a big stink and out the window will go our program. It's been a low-key, non-controversial class and — from everything I've seen or heard — even a little boring for the kids."

"I'll take care of that, Alice."

"I'm sure you will, my dear," she said with a smile. "I'm sure you will, but please be careful about how lively you get."

"Thanks for the advice, pal. I just wish this class had been a part of my job description. It wouldn't have been quite as much of a shock to me if I'd known about it in advance." I took the pile of books from Alice and headed for the door.

"Take those books home, Eric, and study hard," she said to me. "All we need is for you to make some big technical mistake about sperm or fallopian tubes or anything like that and we can kiss the class goodbye!"

My first class with the fifth and sixth grade boys took place two weeks later. I was scheduled to teach eight sessions of human development class, each lasting about fifty minutes. I was assisted in my work by the boy's gym teacher, Chuck Ritter. I had carefully planned an eight-part curriculum that touched all the bases in the syllabus (as well as a few that were glaringly omitted from the syllabus,) and I felt that my preparation was as well done as it could be. I was not, however, confident about teaching this class.

At 1:30 on a Tuesday afternoon, the fifth grade boys came over to my room while the sixth grade girls left for their class with the woman science teacher. I hadn't even thought to challenge the premise behind teaching sex-segregated classes, but when the room was filled with ten- and eleven-year-old guys, I realized that the entire teaching dynamic would be different from my usual class.

I looked up from my desk at the boys sitting around the room. A certain awkwardness prevailed which was subtle and ill-defined. An inordinate amount of tittering was going on — even for this age group. Many of the boys were certainly sitting and gesturing in more "macho" ways than usual. I thought it best to break the ice quickly and begin.

"Today we begin our study of human development," I said speaking slowly, distinctly, attempting to control the nervousness in my voice. "We're teaching this class because we feel it is important for young people to be aware of the changes that take place during the next few years of life. These changes involve physical, emotional and sexual changes and, without any information, could be frightening experiences for you.

"My intent in teaching this class is not to push a certain curriculum on you. I want to know what questions you already have — about sex and sexuality, parts of the body, and the changes that boys and girls go through. I realize that many of you may be a little embarrassed or shy about this discussion and that's okay. So am I. But it's important for us to work through the embarrassment and be able to discuss these topics. Now I want to set the ground rules.

"Nothing that any student says during these discussions goes beyond this room. I want this to be a safe space for people to ask questions, talk about their experiences, share their feelings. It doesn't go to the girls, or to your friends and family outside of the school, and it shouldn't be used to joke about or to tease someone. This is a serious, confidential class and you will have to work with me to keep it that way."

I held up a small cardboard box, about the size of a bread box. "This," I said firmly, "is our question box. It will be in this classroom, at my desk, throughout the weeks we work on this class. It is here so that you can put suggestions in it for the class. If there's a question that you have, something that you didn't understand, or something that you want covered in the next class, write it down and put it in the box. You don't have to sign your name, and no one will know who wrote it. I call it the question box, because I know that some of you will be embarrassed to ask some questions out loud in front of your friends, but if you do have questions, please write them on the cards and put them in the box.

"To begin the class, I will pass out index cards now. I'd like everyone to take out a pen or pencil, and write down any questions on any topic about which you are concerned that is appropriate to this class. I ask you to be honest and serious. Everyone will be expected to put a card into the box. If you cannot think of at least one question, you will have to put a blank card in the box. I'm going to give you about five minutes to think and write and then I'll bring the box around."

The boys took the cards and sat awkwardly, wondering whether to fill them out or deposit them blank. Different boys looked around the room — particularly some of the fifth graders — and, when it became obvious that some people were starting to write on their cards, others began as well. I passed the box around at the end of five minutes and collected the cards. Putting it aside until after school, I launched into my talk about the importance of this kind of education and on how we all learn what we learn about sex and bodily changes. The boys participated, laughing only occasionally, and I was pleased with the discussion. Throughout the dialogue, however, I found my mind racing to that question box and I was curious to see the kinds of questions and the degree of honesty that the boys would exhibit.

It was only after school, when I was alone in the room, that I rifled through the box. I extracted twenty-five cards, most of which were written upon. Only about six or seven were blank, and there was one card with only scribbles. The remaining cards were filled with what appeared to be sincere questions on the minds of these boys.

The questions could be divided into a few categories. Many were what I call the "why?" questions. These included, "Why are babies born without any hair?"; "Why do ladies have breasts?"; and "Why do boys like girls?" Then there were the "what?" and "how?" questions, which included "What exactly is sexual intercourse?"; "How do people do it?"; "What makes boys need to shave?" and "How do people masturbate?" The questions became even more candid. One boy — whose penmanship I recognized immediately, although he attempted to disguise his questions by printing, rather than using his usual script — wrote "What makes boys boys and girls girls?" and "What is a transvestite?"

I put the cards into my backpack and took them home for the evening. I was meeting Paul for dinner in Cambridge, and I looked forward to talking with him about the kinds of questions that my boys seemed to have.

Paul and I met at the Middle-East, a restaurant in Central Square, a bustling, commercial section of Cambridge. When I entered the restaurant a few minutes late, I noticed Paul already seated at a table located near the stage. A belly dancer was writhing her body and undulating her belly. Paul's attention appeared to be riveted on the dancer but upon my approaching the table, he looked up and greeted me.

I smiled back at him and came over. "I find it very amusing that you chose a table so close to the stage," I said sarcastically.

"Did I? We could move if you'd like."

"No, this is fine. I'll just try not to distract you."

Paul went back to looking at the dancer. "I don't think you could even if you wanted to. Just be careful not to block my view."

"Great, I come to have dinner with you and I find myself in the midst of a circus act."

Paul turned back to me. "If you hadn't been twenty minutes late, I'd never be watching. Besides, I'm here to have dinner with you, not watch the dancer. What's up?"

I could tell that, despite his claims, Paul might have some trouble during dinner ignoring the cymbal-clasps and rhythms of the music. Occasionally during our conversation I'd find him looking past me, catch himself, then return and focus his attention on me. I continued talking.

"Paul, I've told you about this sex education course that I have to teach to the fifth and sixth grade boys, didn't I?"

"You sure did. I somehow can't help giggling at the thought of you talking dirty to those kids."

"I can't either," I agreed. "Over the past three weeks I've read everything I could get my hands on."

"Looking for information is one thing, Eric. But you have to find a way to feel comfortable talking about this kind of stuff with kids. That's the real challenge."

"You're right," I agreed. "Because if I come off uncomfortable, it's going to transmit some pretty strong messages to the boys."

"When I first started teaching sex education, I practiced saying some of those hot words out loud. I'd stand in front of the mirror at home and say 'penis' or 'sexual intercourse' or 'vagina' and try not to laugh."

"That sounds like a good idea for teaching technique. Today I had the first class and all we did was talk about sex education in general and I took information from them about the kinds of questions they'd like answered through the class. I'm pretty amazed at the degree of honesty."

"Kids'll surprise you sometimes on this kind of issue."

"I'll say. Do you have any tips about how to handle some of the steamier issues — abortion, contraception, gay issues, and things like the mechanics of intercourse?"

Paul took a piece of pita bread and scooped up some baba ganoosh. "Listen, my friend. My experiences are with older kids, high school age, and I'm not sure how well they'd translate down to your sixth graders."

"Tell me anyway," I said. "I'm desperate for any advice whatsoever."

"I find that the best thing to do is to make the kids comfortable, let them know it's okay to laugh and giggle, but also that it's okay to listen and be serious. Maintaining the proper feeling in the room is probably the most important part of your work. The rest should come from the kids."

"My boys seem to have a lot of questions that don't seem suitable for their age," I confessed.

"What do you mean?"

"Well, some of their questions are about masturbation and shaving and voices cracking and girls' development — all of which seem to be appropriate to their developmental level."

"So what are you concerned about?"

"Some of their other questions get a bit more advanced and seem to arise less from their own bodies and minds, and more from television shows and magazines. Things such as abortion, birth control, sexual intercourse. These kids won't be needing this information for a few years at least."

Paul shoved the plate of hummus over to me and wiped his mouth. "You might be right about some of their questions coming from societal pressures and the media. The fact is, however, that this is where a lot of sex education takes place these days. Whether the course is designed to meet their emotional and physiological needs or designed to answer their honest questions is a question for you to answer. I'd agree with you that the discussions you have about issues that directly affect them — like masturbation — will be most useful."

"Many of them seem to be concerned about gender issues. You know — why boys are boys and girls are girls."

"Does that surprise you?" he asked.

"I suppose it shouldn't but it does."

"Gender issues are key for kids at this age. I'll bet things like cross-dressing and homosexuality and sex roles should be a key part of the program. Who's in charge of the curriculum?"

"I am, I guess," I said as I took a bite from the Greek salad. "I teach it with the assistance of Chuck, the boy's gym teacher whom I've told you about."

Paul smiled. "From what I recall about Chuck, that should insure a mixed perspective in the class. Do you have to answer to anyone in the administration?"

"I guess ultimately I answer to Clarkson and the parents. It's like everything else at the school. The science coordinator is ostensibly in charge of the program, but she's given me free reign while she teaches the fifth and sixth grade girls' program."

"Hey," Paul said, pulling the salad bowl away from me. "Don't pick out all the cheese from the salad! How do you intend to deal with homosexuality in the class? Or, perhaps I should re-phrase that question. *Do* you intend to deal with homosexuality in the class?"

"Of course I do," I insisted. "But I don't really want to do what most of the books I looked at do with the topic. They have a chapter about "other issues" and include birth control, abortion, homosexuality, prostitution, incest, and venereal disease to-gether in one chapter. I think this gives a rather unpleasant cast to homosexuality — to say nothing about what it does for birth control. But I don't really know what else to do."

"Well, one thing I've done, which you might want to consider doing, is focus one particular discussion on gender issues and in-volve homo- hetero- and bisexualities as a part of the discussion. This might be a good way to link the issues and — to be honest — I think the issues are already closely linked in kids' minds al-ready." Paul took a sip of tea and continued. "This might be a good way for you to address their fears and concerns, and also a way to take some of the shock and stigma out of homosexuality. Because, like it or not, this is a topic on all of their minds right now. Who knows? Maybe some of them are already rolling around with each other?"

I thought back to my own sixth grade experiences at Boy Scout camp. "If their experiences are anything like mine," I said, "they're probably already having some pretty hot times. Do you think it would freak them out to talk about these things directly?"

"I think so," Paul said. "I find it difficult and uncomfortable to get boys — or girls, for that matter — to talk about their own experiences too candidly in front of me or their peers, except in a counseling situation. More often, kids talk about their 'close friend who feels this way' or 'someone I know told me . . .' It's difficult for them to openly speak about their experiences."

Getting back to the subject of homosexuality, I asked Paul, "Do you think it's okay if I do just what you suggested — include a section on gender issues which also focuses on sexual orientation — but do it by asking the boys a series of questions first, which could get them thinking. I like to start each class in a unique way that gets the boys engaged and I was thinking of starting with ten questions for them to think about for a few seconds apiece. Questions like, 'What is the difference between boys and girls?' or 'What is a homosexual?' In that way, they could begin thinking about these things and initiate the discussion with their own thoughts and biases. I could then serve to clarify some of the issues for them."

"That sounds okay. Do you have any idea what Chuck will say through this discussion?" Paul asked.

I thought for a second as I finished my meal. "So far, he hasn't said anything," I noted with a smile. "I hope that he'll continue that tradition through the rest of the classes."

Paul's advice was helpful and I focused the next class on gender issues and sexual orientations. The boys' responses to my initial questions indicated that they had a rudimentary knowledge of gender issues and a biased view of homosexuality, but left the door open for discussion. What was most clear to me, from the initial remarks they made, was that they had many uncomfortable feelings and much confusion. We spent the forty-five minute period weaving in and out of the differences between boys and girls, and the things we know — and do not know — about the causes of sexual orientation.

Chuck Ritter did not say a word. He sat through the discussion, watching me carefully throughout, but neither revealing his own thoughts nor contradicting mine. He seemed to be studying the discussion carefully and, more than once, I thought I caught him trying to grasp some of the points that I made. I knew that I was taking risks to raise these issues with Chuck in the room, but

I forged ahead, asking questions, providing information, responding to concerns from the boys.

Perhaps the most difficult part of the discussion surrounding homosexuality was that I could not use my own experiences to illustrate particular points. Nor did I feel comfortable speaking about "gay people that I know," as I did not want to tip my hand. I was relieved when one of the boys raised his hand and brought some real-life experience to the discussion.

It was Stewart Sabinsky — Linda's son — a tall boy with a mouth full of braces, who was popular, athletic, and sociable. When I saw him raise his hand, I called on him immediately. "I have an uncle who's gay," he said, plunging us right into the discussion, "and I don't really think it's such a big deal. He's my father's brother and he's a great guy. He's a lawyer in New York and he lives with this guy, and they come up to visit our family on the holidays. He seems just like a normal man. I mean, he doesn't wear dresses or anything, and he takes me to ballgames when my dad's got to work."

Most of the class was too surprised to respond. I rushed to give Stewart support to discuss the topic further. "How did you find out that your uncle was gay?" I asked.

"I don't remember all the details, but a couple years ago, I guess Jack and some other guys were at my house for a game of football, and my dad heard someone say 'faggot.' He didn't say anything to me at the time but, later, after everyone had gone home, he talked to me about it and said that this wasn't a good word to use because it makes fun of homosexuals and my uncle was one of those.

"I was completely surprised," he continued, "because, at that time, I thought homosexuals were creeps and disgusting, sick people. But my dad helped me to understand why we think those things and he told me not to be prejudiced."

I had to control my joy at hearing these remarks from Stewart; a grin was working its way onto my face and this would not be appropriate. The boy had managed to say everything I'd wanted to say to the group and without any of the adult bias that I would have injected into the discussion. Furthermore, there was no way I could get in trouble for Stewart's remarks.

We continued the discussion for several more minutes and then I brought it to a close. It was an intense, honest discussion and once the bell rang, I was ready for the relief of spelling class.

As the boys got up from their seats to find their way back to their classrooms, I noticed that Stewart's friend Jack remained seated a moment, staring at me blankly and calmly. He had a look on his face that indicated relief. I imagined he'd heard discussion today that related to his personal conflicts and would sustain his sanity and self-worth through some turbulent identity struggles in the coming years.

One Saturday evening during February, I had plans to go dancing with Frank Friedman, a college classmate who, despite our oft--expressed desire to see more of one another, I managed to see only once every few months. During the week before our planned outing, my housemate Gordon hosted his kid brother Ben, down for a visit from the woods of Maine. Within a few quick days, Ben had made a dramatic progression from being casually interested in talking to his big brother's gay housemate to acknowledging his own feelings towards other men. Ben, a strikingly handsome nineteen year old, asked me to take him out for a gay evening on the town. I phoned Frank to see if my new friend could join us and Frank agreed. He suggested we take Ben to Sporters, but I requested another meeting place. I no longer frequented Sporters; the fear of exposure was too great. I'd often see Michael Reich in the corridors of Shawmut Hills and we'd exchange pleasantries about the Parent Committee, but not much more. I consciously kept my distance from him and held firm to the separation between my worlds. That meant giving up Sporters.

Ben and I met Frank for a drink at the Powderhorn, a small, intimate gay bar by the Waterfront, a part of Boston that was practically deserted at night. I had occasionally visited the area with women friends, as this was the location of both Boston's women's bars, and had discovered this quiet drinking place catering to both men and women. Filled with booths and tables, the bar encouraged social discourse and friendliness, and provided board games for its customers. I had become a regular scrabble-player at the bar within a few weeks, and a few of us from the Gay Men's Center regularly made this bar our home.

Ben and I arrived about ten o'clock and settled into a booth. Jacqui Mac, the bartender, came over and greeted us. "How are you doing this evening, fellas?" she asked. "What can I get you?"

I ordered my regular — soda water and orange juice. Ben maintained his Maine, country boy wholesomeness and politely requested a simple glass of water. Frank arrived in a tweed jacket and turtleneck sweater and joined us at the booth, ordering a scotch on the rocks.

When the drinks arrived, Frank looked at Ben's glass of water. "Don't you drink?" he asked.

"Only on a rare occasion," Ben answered. "Liquor does a lot of bad things to me and — aside from a beer every now and then — I've never enjoyed booze much. Plus, when I'm in training for the ski season, I try to maintain a healthy lifestyle."

Frank thought for a moment. "Well, Ben, I'm all for a healthy lifestyle, but I don't see what's wrong with a drink every now and then."

Ben anticipated an argument and became flustered. "For me," he said, "now is not the best time to drink. In addition to it being the ski season, I'm new to these here gay bars and I want to keep my wits about me. I'm kind of nervous and I want to make sure I handle myself like a gentleman."

I noticed Frank looking Ben over. Ben's wholesome looks, square jaw, and powerful build made him an attractive man. He fell outside of every gay stereotype. His boyish smile contrasted with his rugged movements in a way that served as constant reminder that he was a college kid visiting from Maine. Dressed in lumberjack drag, a style popular with urban gay guys, Ben's flannel shirts and workboots were the authentic apparel of his life in the Maine woods, not a contemporary fashion statement. I noted that, in a few days, I had already become very protective of Ben.

"In case I didn't tell you over the phone," I said to Frank, "Ben is new to the scene. In fact, Ben has basically only been with women up to this point."

Ben looked at Frank and said seriously, "I guess I'm what you would call a bisexual, although so far I've only played on one side of the fence. Eric has been mighty helpful to me this week in understanding some of my feelings. I'm not sure that I'm gonna be much of a bar fellow — with all that loud music and smoke — but I'm out to give it a try."

Frank appeared very interested in what Ben had to say. I couldn't tell, as they became involved in their own two-way conversation, whether Frank was interested in Ben because of his dazzling looks, or because Frank was, himself, bisexual and had felt little support for his situation among gay men. Within a few minutes, I wasn't there at all for them, and I found myself gazing around the bar, fiddling with my drink, and moving to the juke box to punch in some music.

As I returned to the table, I noticed out of the corner of my eye two women entering the bar. They passed out of my range of vision quickly, but their laughter and the flash of brown hair somehow struck me instantly. I dashed to my seat, muttering to myself.

Ben and Frank looked up. "What's the matter?" Ben said. "You look like you just saw a ghost."

It took a moment to calm myself to the point of articulateness. "I'm not sure of this," I said tentatively, "but I think that the French teacher from my school just came into this bar."

They looked at me. "So what's so awful about that?" Frank asked. "If she's in the bar, she's got to be a dyke."

"Not this woman," I said. "She's married, sexy and straight as hell. Furthermore, she's probably here because she's got some gay friends, but I haven't told her that I'm gay and I don't want her to find out."

Ben was straining his neck to see them. "Where are they?" he asked. "I don't see any straight ladies."

I turned around to look and realized that they'd walked out of our view, around the corner toward the end of the long bar. "They must've sat down at the end of the bar, over there," I indicated with a point of my finger. "And I can't get up and sneak out without them seeing me."

"Did you get a good look at them?" Frank asked, sipping his scotch.

"Only out of the corner of my eye," I responded. 'But it sure looked like Marie."

"Well, why don't you sneak up to the bar and take another peek?" Frank suggested. "If you go carefully, you can avoid being seen and you can see for yourself if it really is her."

I sat there muttering to myself. "I can't believe I'm in this position," I said. "I'm being ridiculous. What am I afraid of? If she's here, it'll obviously be okay with her. And if it's not her, I have nothing to worry about." Deep inside, however, I felt the tug of my separate worlds colliding.

Ben was the helpful one now. "C'mon, Eric. I'll come up to the bar with you," he said. "We can order another drink from that Jacqui Mac girl, and you can look and see if it's really Miss French Teacher."

I agreed and cautiously slid out of our booth and walked to the bar, making sure that Ben's broad form shielded me from view. As we slid onto two stools at the bar, I glanced beyond Ben. The two women I'd seen enter the club were sitting at the end of the bar, arms around one another, making out. I could see neither of the faces, just a whirl of brown hair, and a hand occasionally grasping out for her drink.

Jacqui came over. "What can I get for you guys now?" she asked, cracking her gum loudly.

I risked appearing nosey. "Listen, Jacqui. I know this sounds strange, but do you know those two women at the end of the bar?"

She glanced over, then looked back at me. "You mean the two that are going at it?"

"Yes, with the brown hair," I answered.

She responded positively. "I know one of them from the bar. She's in here all the time. I've never seen her with this woman before."

"The one you know, is her name Marie? Does she have a French accent?" I asked.

She looked at me and shook her head. "Sorry, Eric," she responded. "Her name is Lois and she's a stockbroker from Wellesley."

I quickly rattled off more questions. "Did you talk to the other one? Does she have big green eyes? Does she have an accent?"

Jacqui poured us the drinks. "Sorry, Eric," she answered again. "I just don't know." Then she gazed again in their direction as she placed our drinks in front of us on the counter. "But, it looks like they're getting ready to leave, so you'll be able to see for yourself."

I grabbed my drink and hurried back to the booth, leaving young Ben at the bar to pay for the drinks. As I skulked down into my seat, pretending to be hidden, I saw the women walk down the length of the bar, past Ben and Jacqui, pulling on their trendy floor-length parkas. While neither woman looked in my direction, one of them — without a doubt — was Marie.

My immediate response surprised me. I froze in my seat, unable to move. Frank looked at me. "So, is she the woman you thought she was?" he asked.

"Yes," I said, slowly. "I can't believe Marie was sitting at the end of that bar, messing around with another woman."

Frank smiled. "Well, why don't you go say hello. If they were making out, that means she's part of the club," he said. "Don't you think it's easier for you to say hello here, than live with this knowledge all the time in school?"

He was right. Summoning up all the courage remaining in me, I left the booth and walked quickly to the door of the bar. As I pushed the door open to enter the vestibule, I noticed the two women by the pay phone. The stockbroker was standing there, wrapping her parka around her, while Marie chatted on the phone, her back toward me.

I wasn't going to stop there. I walked over to Marie and tapped her on the shoulder. Marie was engaged in animated conversation, and continued to speak into the telephone as she slowly turned towards me. As her eyes met mine, they widened suddenly and her mouth opened in shock. "Oh my god," she said into the phone, "It's Eric Rofes."

I smiled back at her. She composed herself quickly and told the party at the other end of the phone connection to hold on for a moment. Covering the receiver tightly with the palm of her hand, she spoke to me.

"Have you been here long?" she asked, attempting to look as innocent as possible.

"Yes, I have," I nodded.

She continued this line of questioning. "Did you see me at the bar?"

I again nodded with a smile. "Yes I did."

"Did you see *everything*?" she asked.

"I don't know, but judging from what I did see, I hope so."

An exasperated look came over her face. She grabbed my shirt with her hand and smiled at me. "I'll be right off the phone. You stay there and don't move."

True to her word, she was off the phone in seconds. She hung up the receiver, turned to me, and threw her arms around my shoulders, burying her face in my chest. As she hugged me, she said, "I can't believe you're here. I can't believe it."

"Let me tell you, sweetheart," I added. "I'm having a hard time believing that you're here."

Then we both burst into laughter.

As the laughter subsided, she put her arm around the stockbroker, who had come over to find out what was going on. "This is my friends Lois," she said to me, and then to Lois she said, "This is Eric Rofes, he's the sixth grade teacher at Shawmut Hills."

I shook Lois' hand and turned back to Marie. "I can't believe you're here. I've never suspected and I've never seen you here before."

"Well, believe it or not," Marie said with a smile, "this is the first time in my life I've been in a gay bar."

Lois chimed in. "And I had promised her that there would be nothing to worry about. Especially at this place, I was sure that we wouldn't run into anyone she knew."

"Are you here with a special friend?" Marie asked, the charming phrasing embellished by her French inflection.

"No, I'm not, but come over and meet my friends." Marie and Lois joined Frank, Ben and me at the table. Jacqui came over to take our orders and to find out what had happened.

She was amused and said, "This kind of thing happens here all the time. A few weeks ago, a guy ran into his wife here."

That made me remember that Marie was married. "But what about your husband?" I asked.

Marie turned to me. "What about him?" she asked.

"Does he know about you?"

"Give me a little time, honey," she said. "Until a month ago, I didn't know about me!"

5

My run-in with Marie at the bar dramatically changed my day-to-day experience at school. Where I once felt alienated and alone, I now felt the comfort that came with having a friend nearby who knew my secret and could empathize with my schizophrenic existence. Marie was someone with whom I could exchange knowing glances at faculty meetings, secret conversations in the corridors between classes, and personal notes laced with euphemisms stealthily passed to one another in the staff room. I began to feel my two selves integrating and experience the relief that comes with letting go of a long-held secret.

Marie and I quickly became friends — both at school and outside of school. I was invited to dinner at Lois' spacious apartment in Lexington, and we'd frequently see one another across the dance floor at Somewhere, a primarily women's bar in the financial district of Boston. I was impressed with their crowd of friends — mostly women like themselves who looked as they did — strikingly attractive, beautifully dressed, professionally coiffed and made up. While my other interactions with lesbians stressed political activism, my time with Marie and Lois was strictly sociable. I even sensed a certain skepticism from the women concerning my involvement in gay community activism.

Throughout the end of the winter, my newfound sense of integration released a surplus of energy for my classroom and my work with the children. Having Marie's friendly face available throughout the school day removed much of the pressure on me and allowed me truly to enjoy my work. I felt good about teaching and was beginning to accept the positive feedback of both parents and Miss Clarkson.

A great deal of my efforts were focused on developing a curriculum for the teaching of the Middle Ages. Throughout the year, my class studied the period from the Fall of Rome to the voyages of Columbus — progressing from the Dark Ages, to the Norman Conquest, to Eleanor of Aquitaine and the Crusades. I had studied this historical period in college and was impressed at the ease of interaction between the historical period and the children's fantasies of King Arthur and Joan of Arc, to say nothing of medieval dragons and monsters. The Middle Ages made up the core of the sixth grade curriculum, and it was my job to bring the period alive for the children.

These are the real challenges facing schoolteachers today. When bigots examine arbitrary factors to determine whether someone would make a suitable teacher, I am struck by their ignorance of the factors that combine to create excellence in education. Whether or not a person can relate to children, present material in an appealing, educational and inspired manner, and generate an excitement and appreciation in young minds for learning seem much more important than sexual orientation or political viewpoint. Creative, talented teachers are rare enough; one need not further limit the pool.

One day, many of the students were working on Middle Ages projects when Miss Clarkson approached me and informed me that she would be observing in my classroom for a while. She had chosen an independent work period for her visit, when the students work in small, autonomous groups on specific projects. A group of boys was working on a model of a medieval village. Some girls were sewing a tapestry modeled after the Bayeaux Tapestry of medieval France, and several others were painting a mural of the costumes of peasants in Old English villages. I traveled from group to group, making suggestions, answering questions, directing the children to specific materials and reference books which could help their projects maintain a close relationship to historical fact. The end of the school day was approaching, so I called on the students to end work early, allowing them ample time to clean up. I directed them back to their seats for final assignments.

After dismissal, Miss Clarkson came up to my desk to speak with me. "I must say, Eric," she began, looking after the students as they departed. "I am impressed with the projects that are developing in this room. The children seem genuinely enthusiastic about their work and seem to be learning quite a bit about the Middle Ages."

"I'm glad to hear that, Miss Clarkson," I responded candidly. "I'm always nervous when you observe in the classroom and, since this wasn't a time when I was teaching a lesson at the front of the room, I wasn't sure you'd get a full sense of what we do here."

"I continue to get calls," she said, "from parents who are concerned about some of the more experimental aspects of your program. However, I feel more and more comfortable all the time telling them that your overall program is strong, and that the children are learning a great deal. My only concern is whether or not the material they are learning and your methods of teaching allow them to gain the skills they will need to do well on the achievement tests they take in two weeks. These tests will be forwarded to their next school and will — in large part — determine where the children are placed in mathematics, English, and other classes."

I was already concerned about these exams. I knew full well that, regardless of how creative and enjoyable my program was — and how much the children were learning and growing — unless they scored well on these tests, their parents would succumb to doubts about the program. Formalized testing seemed designed simply to validate parental apprehensions and to discount the strengths of any teacher's curriculum which could not possibly be quantified through testing.

"To be perfectly honest with you," I said to Miss Clarkson, "I am concerned about the tests too. I feel that I've prepared the children for them as well as I could, without allowing the tests to determine my entire curriculum for the year. At this point, all I can do is hope for the best."

"Well, for the sake of the children — as well as your program," Miss Clarkson agreed, "I too hope for the best." She turned and, with a controlled smile on her face, walked quickly down the hall.

One day, as I was collecting homework from the students, Ann approached my desk, her fingers nervously pulling at the ends of her pigtails. I looked up from the papers and asked what she wanted.

Tossing her hair quickly behind her shoulders, in a quiet, guilt-ridden voice, Ann confessed, "My homework's not ready. I wasn't feeling well last night and my mother made me go to bed early."

I had heard this excuse earlier that week from Ann and my patience was wearing thin. I held what I considered to be high, yet appropriate, standards for the children. A child like Ann could be expected to complete her homework and, at least three times during the past few days, she had managed to create similar excuses.

"Ann," I spoke quietly but sternly to her. "This is the fourth time this week you haven't done your homework. Is something going on that I should know about that is keeping you from doing your work?"

She looked down at her feet and shuffled uncomfortably. "I just told you," she said. "I wasn't feeling well last night and my mother made me go to bed."

"But you had time to catch up on the homework before school today. You arrived here a half an hour early, and all I saw you do was chat with your friends and write notes." I could tell that I was getting angry and excited and a hush came over the room as the other students anticipated the scene to come. "I cannot accept another excuse from you about not doing your homework, Ann. I want you to stay in during lunch time recess and finish your vocabulary."

Then I turned to the rest of the class. "Homework is due when I say it is due. This does not mean that I will not allow for illness or change of family plans or the homework being too difficult for you. It does mean that I expect you to try to get help, and try to find the time to do it. If there is a regular problem with assignments, I will have to contact your parents and try to find out what is going on."

Ann walked back to her seat, keeping her chin her on chest. I could tell that she was about to cry. She put her head on her desk and covered it with her arms and I began to review the assignment with the rest of the class.

I had been too harsh with the girl and I knew it. Something was going on in her life that was keeping her from her work and my yelling was not going to change the matter. I had chosen the wrong approach to use with her. Instead of being encouraging and supportive, I had been rigid and angry.

This had been a long-term issue for me. I had wrestled with finding a way to be warm and supportive to my students while maintaining appropriate standards of discipline and high academic expectations. That was not always easy to achieve, particularly since my physical appearance was intimidating to many children. As a tall, dark, bearded man, I appeared to them as a frightening authority figure and I had to work to break down the barriers that made me seem unapproachable. My greatest liability for working with young people was my temper and, while I made a conscious attempt to control it, and to employ a loud voice only on rare occasions, this was clearly an area in which I needed improvement.

In this situation, I hadn't realized how much I'd upset Ann until I found the note at the end of the day:

Dear Mr. Rofes,

Please don't yell at me in class for not doing my homework. *Please* do it in private! But I have what I think are very good reasons. After school I went to Monica's. I had no free moment till 5:30 and then I found out we were going skiing. I had to go because: 1. it was a family trip; 2. nobody could stay with me. We were busy from 5:30 A.M. till 8:00 P.M. and after dinner I fell right to sleep! Please don't yell in class. Yell at me privately and give me Friday Detention then, if you must, but privately *please*. If possible, which I doubt, could you try to give me an extra day? Oh, you might say that I must have had some free time. I had a night full of a bad stomach ache. But please don't embarrass me in front of my friends. I'd rather have Friday Detention instead. Please take my plea!

> Sincerely,
> Ann

P.S. I did start the story or tried at about five this morning, but I fell asleep. Please, I'd rather die or have Friday Detention instead of being embarrassed in front of my friends.

After reading the letter, I immediately walked down the hall and showed it to Marie. She read it slowly and then looked up at me. "You didn't yell at her in front of her friends, did you?" she asked, looking me directly in the eye.

I was stricken with guilt. "As a matter of fact, Marie, I did," I confessed. "I can see now that it wasn't a good thing to do, but I admit that I did it and I feel awful."

"Sit down, ma cheri," Marie said. I sat in the chair next to her desk. Since it belonged to her second grade French students, my large frame stuck out on all sides. The child chair made me feel more like a foolish kid that I already did.

Marie continued, "One of the things it's important for you

new teachers to realize is that kids have feelings too. It's not a good idea to humiliate them in public. This is the worst punishment that can be held against a sixth grader — especially a sixth grade girl. Don't you remember what that felt like when you were a youngster?"

I remembered my fifth grade teacher, Mr. Amundsem, and how he once embarrassed a classmate so often in public that the boy — usually a rather rational sort of guy — went beserk in the classroom and started knocking over the furniture and throwing books. We didn't see the boy for days and, after he returned to school, he was never again the same in our eyes.

"I suppose that I shouldn't have done that, and I owe Ann an apology," I admitted.

"I think so," Marie said. "But don't feel that awful about it. This is what my first few years of teaching were about. I needed to make some mistakes and learn from them. I think that you're the kind of fellow who can admit his mistakes. Most teachers can't."

"The last line of this note is what really gets to me," I said, reading through Ann's note again. "She writes, 'I'd rather die or have Friday Detention instead of being embarrassed in front of my friends.' I suppose that, to these kids, having Friday Detention is comparable to an early death, but it does highlight the intensity of her feelings about public humiliation."

"Yes, it does," Marie agreed. She got up from her seat, walked around behind me, and put her hand on my shoulder. "But don't let this worry you too much. You've learned an important lesson, Ann hasn't died, and in a few days, after you apologize, you and she will be back to business as usual. Just promise me one thing."

"What's that?"

"That you'll continue to set limits for those kids and won't let this single incident intimidate you. They need someone who won't take their excuses. You just have to find a way to set the limits that is more humane. Now promise me you'll keep at it, teacher."

I walked to the door with the note in my hand and turned to

Marie. "I promise. I'll set firm standards and cause no more public humiliation," I said, and walked down the corridor to my classroom.

Before school the next day, I tried to talk with Ann. She came into the classroom early and quietly took her seat, then took out her notebook and began reading some of her notes. Every time I attempted to meet eyes with Ann she averted hers. Finally, I put down my pen, pushed my chair back, got up and approached her desk.

"Good morning, Ann," I said in a quiet voice.

"Good morning, Mr. Rofes," she said without looking up.

I continued quietly, "I would very much like to have a short chat with your right now, if you can take the time out of your studying to come into the reading room for a few minutes."

Ann didn't react for a moment. Then she closed her binder tightly and, keeping her eyes averted, walked to the back of the classroom to the reading room. I followed her, aware that other students arriving in the classroom had their eyes glued on this action. I entered the reading room, closed the door behind me, and took a seat.

"Please sit down," I said, gesturing at a seat.

She sat, eyes still firmly set to the ground.

I took a deep breath and began, "I received your note yesterday at the end of school. I have been very upset since reading it and I feel badly that I embarrassed you in front of the rest of the class. That was the wrong thing for me to do and I promise you that I will never do it again. I don't think I realized how painful that kind of punishment can be to children at your age."

I paused to give Ann a chance to respond. She maintained her stony gaze and offered no response. I continued nervously. "You have every right to be angry at me and you may decide that what I did was so bad that you'll never forgive me, but I hope that you'll understand that even teachers make mistakes and that when someone apologizes and acknowledges a big mistake that it's important to try and be forgiving."

Ann still said nothing. I was beginning to feel very uncomfortable and run out of ideas for drawing her out. I decided to change tack and ask a question. "When do you think would be a good time for me to expect your story?" I asked.

Ann immediately looked up at me. "Do I still have to do the story?" she asked, obviously surprised by my question.

"Did you expect that because of my apology that I was going to forget about the story?" I asked.

"Well," she began, "I was kind of hoping that you'd feel guilty enough to tell me to forget it." She began smiling. "I was hoping that you'd act like you were doing me a big favor by saying that I didn't have to hand in the story. Then I was planning on saying, 'Thank you' and opening up my binder like this, taking out my paper, like this, and saying to you, 'But, Mr. Rofes, I've already finished it, so you'll have to grade it anyway.' Then I was going to walk out of the room."

"Well," I said, "I'll do whatever you'd like at this point. If you want me to pretend you didn't tell me all that, I'll waive the requirement for the paper."

Ann got out of her seat. "Listen," she said. "Here's my paper. Promise you'll never embarrass me again in front of my friends and I'll promise to be better with homework assignments. The next time I'm late, you can give me Friday Detention. Okay?"

I took the paper from her and looked it over. It appeared to be long, carefully and neatly written, and was entitled "The Angry Teacher." "Okay, Ann," I agreed. "Next time, no humiliation, just Friday Detention."

The upcoming achievement tests asserted an unspoken pressure on my students throughout the early spring. Knowing that their status in their next schools would be determined by these tests, my class appeared more irritable, nervous, and self-conscious than usual. While the students were never explicitly informed about the use to which these tests would be put, an awareness permeated the classroom. As I discussed the upcoming exams with the class, I tried to dispel their fears. Their questions, however, clearly revealed the causes for their concerns.

After explaining the kinds of questions that would be on the test and assuring the students that they were well prepared, I opened up the discussion to questions.

Several hands shot up. I called on Monica first.

"Mr. Rofes. You said that we should relax about these tests and that we were already well prepared for them, but my parents told me that I should study hard for them," she said. She opened her desk top and pulled out an oversized paperback book. "They even bought me this study guide, about basic skills, and they've been making me do ten pages in it every night. Is this going to help me?"

"I don't want to contradict anything your parents might tell you and using that book certainly won't hurt you. I'm not sure, however, that studying will be of much help. I am afraid, however, that too much studying might make you more nervous than you'd be anyway and this could work against you. On the other hand, I do think it's important for you all to be familiar with the kinds of questions which will be on the tests, which is why tomorrow we will go over some sample questions."

Arthur spoke next. "Is all that work we did on vocabulary and spelling this year going to help us at all?" he asked.

"I hope so," I responded. "A lot of the test is focused on basic language skills, and I think the work we've done this year on vocabulary, spelling, writing, reading, and memorization of rules will help you."

"Should we study our notes?" he asked.

"That might be a good idea, but again, I wouldn't spend too much time preparing for this test. I can't tell you exactly what will be covered, because it's different every year. I can't promise you that your specific vocabulary words will help you."

"What will happen if we fail these tests?" asked Stewart, who was bright enough not to need to worry, although he was always concerned about failing tests.

"The only thing these tests might affect is the level of placement in math or reading in seventh grade," I answered. "You've already been accepted or rejected at specific schools. This won't change those decisions. They will only affect placement."

I looked up at the clock. "It's almost dismissal time," I said. "I don't want you to spend a lot of time thinking about these tests. I expect that you'll do very well. Please try not to lose any sleep over them and I hope that your folks don't lose any either." I began to pass out a notice. "This sheet is intended for your parents and it will give them the same kind of information I gave you. You'll also notice, on the bottom, that I remind them that they should try not to pressure you about these tests. I hope that it helps."

April arrived and my daily walk up Shawmut Hill was brightened by the appearance of buds on the trees and daffodils springing up from along the driveways that emptied into Shawmut Hills Road. While April in the Boston area brings the uncertainty of whether or not we've seen the last of the bitter weather, this year spring seemed filled with optimism, warmth, and the promise of a three-month summer vacation.

The achievement tests came and went without a great deal of fanfare. Standardized tests are always much heralded in advance, yet seem to arrive in an anticlimactic whirl. For all the pain and struggling and fears the children endure for weeks ahead of time, exam day is routine, rigorous, and without immediate conse-quences or results. Test scores don't arrive until almost a month or so later and the individual students are left in a waiting-stage between having done the best they could in taking the test and not yet knowing the results. By the time the grades are flown out of Princeton, and arrive at school, most students have buried their fears and anticipations in the backs of their minds.

On May Day, the school held an annual celebration, com-plete with Maypole dance, songs, dramas, and recitations. All the classes met in the schoolyard and joined in the festivities, cele-brating the arrival of springtime and the departure of winter. Our woolen sweaters served as reminders that the freedom of summer was still weeks away, but the smell of freshly-cut grass filled us with the exhilaration of the day.

As we walked out to the playing fields to observe some of the day's dramatic performances (fourth grade was performing an Egyptian play; third grade had prepared some skits based on Greek myths), Miss Clarkson approached and pulled me aside. "I've just gotten word that the exam grades have arrived," she said in a hushed voice. "I'll look them over right after assembly ends. Can you stop down to my office around ten-thirty. I believe you have a free period then."

Sensing the excitement in her voice — one of the rare times one could sense genuine verve from the headmistress of Shawmut Hills — I readily agreed. "Does this mean the parents will be receiving their grades today as well?" I asked.

"There's usually a one or two day lapse," she answered. "Princeton seems to send them to schools on one day and the parents on the next — probably to give us time to prepare for parental response. And if this year's like previous years, there are always at least three or four surprise disappointments. Those parents tend to phone the school right away and come in to meet with us. It takes a major counseling job to calm everyone."

A nine-year-old Cleopatra was about to make her entrance with a rubber asp. "I see the play's about to start," Miss Clarkson observed. "We'll chat more at ten-thirty."

The skits went longer than expected. Diminutive King Tuts and Queen Nefertitis, Atlases and Aphrodites, as well as several assorted gods with wings on their backs and feet, kept the crowd amused, but I remained preoccupied with the test results. After assembly, I marched the class back to classroom, taught my reading lesson then hurried down to the office.

I found the door ajar. I knocked quietly, to no response. I knocked again, a bit louder, and was greeted by a distracted voice, telling me to come in and close the door.

Miss Clarkson sat at her desk, fully absorbed in a mass of papers before her. The faculty often joked that her office was furnished in "modern swamp" style. Although the school crest included a lamb, years ago, Miss Clarkson had let her personal preference for turtles be known. For twenty years, gift after gift given to her by graduating students and their families had been chosen around this theme. I glanced around the room at the turtle paper-weights, turtle pillows, turtle planters, and framed turtle wall-hangings. There was a turtle stool, books about turtles, and an aquarium filled with tiny turtles. For relief, I looked out of the windows, past the turtle-print curtains, at the full-flowering of springtime in the schoolyard. I felt nervous.

Miss Clarkson finally looked up and noticed me. "I'm sorry I appear to be so absorbed in these results, Eric," she said. "I wanted to be sure I had fully read through them before I presented them to you. The scores are rather surprising, and you and I have a great deal to talk about if we are to be prepared for parental response tomorrow."

Miss Clarkson's voice became serious in tone. "I can't say that the results surprise me. You've taught the sixth grade this year with some very — how shall we put it — novel and experimental teaching techniques. As much as things seemed to be going well throughout the year, one could never be sure exactly what or how much the children were learning. These results are, in fact, the first clear evaluation of the success of your methods of teaching."

It didn't sound good and I feared the worst. Miss Clarkson got up from her desk and sat in the chair beside me so that, together, we could look over the scores.

"Looking at these results," she said, "one has to acknowledge the tremendous success you've had with your class this year These results generally tend to correlate with the tests taken by these same children at the end of their fifth grade year. On comparing your students' scores last year with their scores this year, there is an overwhelming improvement. I find this quite remarkable.

"Let's look at Arthur's scores, for example," Miss Clarkson said, taking out the test result sheet from last year and setting it next to this year's results. "Arthur's a bright boy, and last year finished ahead of 81% of all students who took the test nationwide on verbal skills and ahead of 91% in math. This year he is at 94% verbally and 98% in math. This is signficant improvement."

She continued, "But when you look at a girl who is generally not a strong achiever, such as Ann, the results are also impressive. Last year she had a 41% in verbal and a 35% on the mathematics. This year her verbal rose to 65% and her math to 78%. Again, a significant — one might even say astounding — improvement."

I looked over the full sheet of test results, my eyes darting for comparisons to the fifth grade score sheet. Almost every score had risen impressively. I breathed a sigh of relief.

"Are the tests that the children are administered in the fifth grade the same test as they were given this year?" I asked.

"No, Eric," she answered, "They are given grade-level tests every year, hence we generally don't see such major leaps as we do this year.

"There are some disappointments," she continued. "If you look at Monica's scores, for example, they appear to be much lower than one would expect. She's at 75% and 78%. But this has been her situation for years. This is simply a girl that does not do well on standardized tests."

"Are her folks aware of this?" I asked, imagining Monica's fiery mother storming the school after seeing the results.

"Well, they've been getting accustomed to it, and they were really hoping for improvement this year. Looking at Monica's scores from last year, it seems clear that there has been an improvement, but perhaps not as great an improvement as we would have hoped for."

Miss Clarkson arose and assumed her seat behind her desk. "Despite a few disappointments," she said, "you should feel pleased with the results. They are truly impressive and they should serve as a complete vindication of your program to those parents who have been concerned about your methods. I am personally very heartened by the results."

I sat there, still a bit struck by the news. "Well," I said slowly, "I'm very happy with this news. It comes as a tremendous relief to me."

"It should," she said, folding up the papers. "I must ask you one thing. Please do not 'leak' these results, before the children receive their formal notification. Even to the rest of the faculty. Many teachers are friendly with the parents. I'd like this to be a pleasant May surprise for the families, and for yourself."

I rose again to depart. "Again, Eric," Miss Clarkson said, "I couldn't be more pleased with these results. Congratulations on your fine work with the children this year."

I returned to my empty classroom elated. It was frustrating that I wasn't able to announce this news to the kids and the faculty, but I decided that Marie could keep a secret, so I walked down the hall to the French classroom. She was sitting at her desk, grading papers, when I arrived.

"What's up, big boy?" she asked with a smile.

"Can I close the door?" I asked.

She looked surprised. "People will talk, sweetheart," she said sarcastically.

I closed the door tightly, then walked back to her desk. "The achievement test results came in today," I announced.

"Has Clarkson shown them to you yet?" she asked with interest.

"I've just spent the last half hour in her office, going over the results for my class," I answered.

"And — ?"

"The results are wonderful. The kids seem to have done impressive work on these tests and even Clarkson is struck by their improvement over last year's tests," I was talking a mile a minute. "She even said to me 'Congratulations on your fine work with the children this year,' " I said in my best high-brow imitation of Clarkson's voice.

"Well, this sounds like cause for celebration. Did you bring the champagne?"

"Almost all of the kids made tremendous improvements," I said, "And Clarkson thinks this is very unusual and a 'vindication' of my teaching methods."

"Bravo, Eric!" Marie said. "After all the pressure on you this year, I'm glad to hear that you turned out to be correct."

I thought for a moment. "You know, the strange thing is, I was all prepared for these tests not to make any difference to me. You know, that education happens in the classroom and can't be evaluated by standardized tests and all that. The things that you and I have been saying all year. I think I'm putting a little too much emphasis on these results."

Marie stared at me. Then she got up from her seat, walked over to me, put her hands on my shoulders and shoved me into a second-grade seat.

"Now you listen to me, mister," she said in a stern voice. "I'm not going to let your militant views of education keep you from enjoying the results of these tests. The fact of the matter is that your students seem to have done very well and you deserve a large part of the credit, particularly after all you've been through this year. In fact," she said, looking at her watch, "after school today, I'm taking you out for a celebration. I'll call Lois and we'll take you out to dinner. Does this fit in with your evening plans?" she asked.

I thought for a minute. "I guess so," I said. "But isn't this going a little too far?"

"Nothing is too far when Clarkson has something so extremely nice to say about a teacher. In fact," she said with a smile, "I think we'll have to call the newspapers as well. This really is history in the making."

The last months of a school year seem to rush by and, before I knew it, we were entering our final days of the term. I spent Memorial Day with a friend, double dating with Marie and Lois in Provincetown — my first visit to the Cape Cod resort.

Returning from the weekend, we rushed through final exams, final reports, and final classes, and I found myself standing in the back of the school's auditorium, watching my twenty-five sixth graders graduate from Shawmut Hills School. As Miss

Clarkson read off their names, spoke of their accomplishments, and awarded each student a diploma, my mind wandered back to the early days of the school year. Remembering the little boys and girls that had arrived in September, I was struck by their growth over one short school year. As they stood on the stage, singing (off-key) those graduation songs that seem written precisely to bring tears to a teacher's eyes, they no longer seemed to be children. They had become young men and women, ready to tackle all the issues that come with the entrance into junior high school. As the curtain came down, the graduates rushed haphazardly off the stage, and I felt a hand on my shoulder.

Turning, I saw that it was Linda Sabinsky, tears streaming down her face. "Eric," she said. "Thanks for giving our kids the best damn year they've ever had." Her arms encircled my shoulders and she hugged me to her. At that moment, all the late-night phone calls, the tension surrounding achievement tests, and the crazy curriculum debates of the school year seemed worthwhile.

Michael Reich was there in his role as chairman of the Parent Committee. He came up and shook my hand. I immediately stiffened at the proximity of this man who single-handedly had kept me out of my favorite gay bar for eight months. I caught myself, remained relaxed and greeted him awkwardly with what came out as a flirtatious smile.

"Congratulations on surviving your first year at Shawmut Hills," he said, returning my grin. "Beatrice tells me you'll be returning next year and I'm sure that's good news for the school."

"Thanks very much, Michael," I said somewhat awkwardly.

"Sometime in the fall, let's get together and talk. I've been a little lax in my duties here and I feel as if you're the one teacher who I haven't gotten to know very well. I'll give you a call in September."

As he walked away, I breathed a silent sigh of relief.

Parent after parent came up to extend their thanks and appreciation. Several had brought little wrapped gifts for me, which I placed in a pile on my desk to open after the keyed-up emotions had calmed down. Annette Green took my hand said, "Thanks for the good year. I look forward to seeing you in another two years, when my little Johnnie is in sixth grade. Until then," she said with a big wink, "*do* keep in touch."

My students also came up to shake my hand, or tearfully hug me goodbye. I sensed their feelings of conflict at having to leave the school they'd come to consider home over the past six or seven years. They were taking a step outward, enlarging their world, anticipating the excitement and fears that lay before them.

As I sat at my desk after the ceremony, feeling emotionally drained, looking out over the twenty-five empty seats, the bulletin boards cleared of displays, the books sorted and lined up against the classroom cabinets, I too felt the wrench of separation. A knock at the door broke my mood, and I saw Alice standing outside. I motioned for her to enter. She entered, carrying a big box of cookies in one hand, and a pile of books in the other.

"Well, Eric, you've gotten through your first year. I brought some cookies to celebrate with," she said, extending the box, "and some books for your summer curriculum work," she added, placing the pile before me. Then she looked into my eyes. "How you doing, kid?" she asked warmly.

"Alice, do teachers have a tougher time with their first graduation than the others?" I asked.

"Feeling sad, are you?" she asked, taking a cookie. "Your first class will always be special to you, and their graduation's going to hit you the hardest. Are you surprised at what you're feeling?"

I thought for a moment. "I guess not," I answered. "But when I took this job, I didn't think about how I'd feel now. You spend a year putting all this emotional energy into a group of kids and then they graduate and you never see them again."

"It's like being a parent and watching your kids move out and leave you," Alice said quietly. "Except as a teacher, it happens every year, and you have twenty-five kids leaving home."

Alice continued. "You should feel very satisfied, Eric. I'll bet you're too exhausted now to think about the year ahead, but I know many of the fifth graders are excited about moving up. It's a lively class, so I think you'll have your hands full. You'd better rest up this summer and recharge your batteries. What are your plans for the summer anyway?"

My mind went blank for a moment and then I remembered that this was going to be a summer of a lot of involvement in the Gay Men's Center and *Gay Community News*. I thought for a minute, and then I lied, "I'm not sure yet what I'm up to, but I know I'm going to have fun, get a lot of rest, and probably get into a little trouble."

"Well," Alice said as she moved toward the door. "After the year we've put you through, you deserve all the rest you can get. And as far as trouble goes, keep my number handy. After surviving three sons, I've developed some skills at dealing with trouble. When the cops tell you you've got one phone call, remember Alice."

The year had been good for me. I felt like a competent young professional, my twenty-two-year-old life about to burst into action. The promise of a satisfying teaching career, and support from parents and faculty, made me look hopefully at the next year. My one great fear involved my growing activism. Would I be able to sustain my interest in the education of children and retain my teaching job as I felt compelled more and more to speak out, and become involved in politics? How would I mesh my personal life, my gay activism, and my professional responsibilities? Could I continue to maintain the separation of my two lives, or would this division tear me apart?

This conflict became more clear about a week after graduation. My friends from the *Gay Community News* had been urging me to join them in the annual Gay Pride Parade in Boston. Every part of me wanted to be there, in the streets, as part of that celebration, yet I feared being spotted, picked up by television cameras, and my schoolteacher face splashed onto the television screen. I wrestled with the mixed emotions I felt, until I arrived at a solution.

The march began at noon on a brilliant, sunny Saturday in

Boston's Copley Square. The street was a collage of people, floats, colorful balloons, and flowing banners. As the organizers urged people to line up behind the lead banner, chants could be heard: "Say it loud, gay and proud!", "2-4-6-8, How do you know your husband's straight?", "3-5-7-9, lesbians are mighty fine!" Thousands of men, women and children ambled into place, smiling, cheering, laughing together. Farmers from Vermont joined lawyers from Cambridge. Gay youth marched alongside lesbian grandmothers. One woman, dressed in a clown costume, juggled five oranges and wore a bright pink t-shirt proclaiming "Lesbian Clown."

The march stepped off at 12:30 and there I was, standing among three thousand smiling souls that day, enjoying the thrill of my first Pride Parade. Wearing a paper bag over my head, with holes cut through for my eyes, nose and mouth, I carried a large sign, reading "Dick and Jane have come out. Their teachers can't. Gay Rights Now!"

The excitement of marching down Boylston Street, waving at throngs of spectators, was overwhelming.

As the march passed the Arlington Street Church — long a center for social movements in Boston — the bells pealed and bright pink banners unfurled from the steeple, reading "Happy Gay Pride!" The excitement of the day, the heat of the afternoon, and the surrounding joy at being out there on the street among thousands of others, combined to make the paper bag on my head hot, sweaty, and unbearable. As the parade turned onto Charles Street and began its procession through Beacon Hill, I noticed two striking brown-haired women on the side of the street, gazing intently at my sign. Recognizing Marie and Lois, I began to wave my hand wildly, then my sign, and then, in one deft movement, I reached up and pulled the bag triumphantly off my head and tore it to pieces.

6

Any school teacher can tell you that summer vacation passes with the speed of light. Once all final responsibilities are completed, reports for the past terms are filed, and supplies for the coming year are ordered, a schoolteacher is in a state of exhaustion which lingers until Labor Day weekend. The hazy weeks between June graduation and September start-of-classes rush by at breakneck speed. Before I knew it, I was back at school, with new books, new supplies and new students. Once again, colorful construction paper leaves adorned the bulletin board outside my classroom.

Independent school teaching has its advantages and disadvantages compared to public education. The chief disadvantage is the embarrassingly small salaries (I was making $8,000 in my second year), and the chief advantage is greater teacher control over curricular matters and teaching technique. Part of my summer had been spent drafting my own text for use in the Middle Ages class and I returned to Shawmut Hills excited about using the book with my students. I was also looking forward to a women's studies course I was initiating in the school, as well as this year's holiday play, which would be based on the Robin Hood stories.

With new materials and new programs — to say nothing of my new students — I looked ahead to an exciting year.

When my class filed into the classroom and took their seats, I was struck by the size of the group. Teaching a class of eighteen students is worlds apart from teaching twenty-five, and I felt relieved with the size of the class. I was concerned, however, with the fact that I only had three girls in my class. On the first day of school, a one to five ratio of girls to boys did not look promising, especially to a teacher planning to teach a course in women's studies.

Later that morning, I found myself sitting alone with Marie in the staff room. "So, Mr. Eric," she said, a hint of teasing already in her voice. "Are you planning on an 'active' school year?"

I didn't know what she was getting at and she sensed my confusion from the look on my face.

"By 'active,' my dear, I mean are you still involved in those *gay* activities? When Lois and I saw you in Provincetown in July, you told us you were working with this youth group, and I know you're still writing for the gay newspaper — I see your pseudonym all the time. What do you have planned for this year?" she asked.

"I'm not really sure if there'll be any more excitement," I said. "I am still working with the Committee for Gay Youth — that support group for gay teenagers we've talked about — and I still write for *Gay Community News*. The one group I'd like to see started this year is a support group for gay teachers." I looked at Marie. "Interested in getting involved?" I asked.

She shook her head. "Not me. You know me, I'm not a joiner."

"Well, I'll let you know when and if anything happens. You might want to come to a meeting at some point."

Marie looked doubtful. "It'll be quite a chilly day in hell before you get this gal to go to a meeting of a gay teachers group." She paused before continuing and took a sip from her coffee cup. "But I do admire your youthful enthusiasm, and I wish you well. Please keep me informed of what's going on."

"What do *you* have planned for this year?" I asked.

"Now that Ron and I have formally separated, everything is a lot easier for Lois and me. I'm planning on being a great French teacher, keeping my sweetie warm at night, and going skiing as often as weather and time permit," she answered.

Just then the door banged open. In came Chuck Ritter, who'd spent his summer coaching basketball at a boy scout camp.

"What's this I hear about skiing?" he bellowed. "If someone in here's planning to go skiing without me, they have something coming to them."

Marie and I looked at one another. "Listen, Chucky," she said with a smile. "I'm the one who's planning on doing the skiing this year, and if you ever want to join my friends and me, that's fine with us."

"Great," he exclaimed. "Just give me a day's warning and I'll come along."

"There's one thing you should know," she said with a serious face. "We're all girls and you might have a difficult time keeping up with the gossip at the pajama parties. Still, Chucky, I think you'd look adorable with your hair all in curlers!"

The ski season arrived early and I saw less and less of Marie and Lois as they ventured north each weekend to New Hampshire. My second year as a teacher rushed forward in a blur of meetings, classes, parent conferences and grading papers. Between my hectic school life and my active "extra-curricular activites" — as I grew to call my activism — I was busy constantly and had little time to assess my situation.

Alice had been correct that my first class of students would always be special to me. I spent a great deal of the fall comparing my classes and noting distinctions and shortcomings that made my new students initially seem less appealing. Teaching was easier, however, the second time around. In addition to the fewer students (seven fewer essays each week, seven fewer spelling tests . . .) and the greater curricular resources I'd amassed, my teaching skills were honed and I was beginning to work efficiently and quickly on my teaching duties.

This allowed me the time to throw myself into my "other" life. I was now regularly writing major articles for the newspaper and coordinating a monthly speakers' series for the Gay Men's Center. I was also falling in love — which proved to be quite time consuming — with a beautiful, dark Italian man from Boston's North End. Tony Mosca was showing me a life I'd never dreamed of living at twenty-three — dinners at fine restaurants, weekends by the shore, cultured, sociable friends. I fell head-over-heels for this man, ignoring the age difference between us — he was thirty-two — as well as the central fact of his existence. Tony was a Catholic priest.

Loving a priest is not a picnic, but throughout the waning months of the year, I easily overlooked the problems. Sharing the Christmas holidays with Tony's clan was a special treat for me as I was learning to eat spicy Italian cooking and observe new ethnic customs. I envied the tacit acceptance of Tony's homosexuality by his family who — while never defining or categorizing or stating in words what was obvious — welcomed me as a son. And I was struck by the exhiliration of pulling blankets up over two big men on a cold winter evening and snuggling all night long. When Tony would tiptoe out at dawn to hurry to the seven o'clock mass, he'd kiss me on the forehead and set the alarm. I felt loved and cared for by another man — for the first time.

It wasn't until January that I had time to sit back and look at my life and acknowledge that each piece of the puzzle that comprised my identity was actually in good shape. My love life was satisfying, my career felt successful, my political work was escalating, and my friends kept me honest. In the back recesses of my mind, though, I had a growing sense that somehow my sense of satisfaction would not continue unchallenged. I was coping well with the stresses that accompanied the situation, but I was beginning to be aware that such stress took its toll. I attended a local television show debate on gay rights and had a very difficult time not participating in the debate. Nevertheless, several students and their parents saw me in the studio audience and I felt the clash of my two worlds again. Their total assumption of my heterosexuality kept me safe for the time, but I was beginning to realize that either the activism had to be kept under strict limits or I'd have to leave teaching.

During winter vacation, Paul and I took a trip to Provincetown for a few days, pretending we had the money to travel far away on a major vacation. We shared a room at Land's End Inn, a cozy guest house in a remote corner of town set high atop a hill overlooking the very tip of Cape Cod. For three days we talked education, ate hearty meals at the few restaurants that remained open, and read novels sitting under blankets before the fireplace. It was a relaxing vacation, intended to prepare us for the winter semester.

On the long drive back from Provincetown on Sunday evening, we ran into heavy snow. Paul switched on the wipers and I turned on the radio. Forecasters were predicting a major storm.

Paul turned and looked at me, a mischievous smile coming over his face. "Are you thinking what I'm thinking?" he asked.

"What are you talking about?"

"Come on, you're a schoolteacher."

"I don't know what you're getting at," I insisted, getting irritated at his immaturity.

"Isn't your mind racing with visions of a snow day?" Paul asked, his eyes twinkling.

The thought had yet to pass through my mind. As we sped up the highway toward Boston, the snow began to accumulate on the roads. The possibility of a snow day did not seem remote. "Just get me home safely," I said to Paul, as we watched other cars skid and slide from side to side. "I've got my lesson plans to finish for tomorrow and I'd really appreciate it if my head were intact."

I arrived home, finished my schoolwork, and went to bed that night filled with nervous anticipation. Weather forecasters in Boston frequently predict massive snowfalls that never materialize. Few people realize that schoolteachers and children are awake at five in the morning to see whether the dire predictions have come true. As I tossed and turned in bed throughout the night, my mind was filled with excitement. Would winter vacation be extended a day due to massive snowfall? Would I have an extra day to prepare my classes, read the necessary background material, and hang out around the house?

As could have been predicted, I awoke at five and immediately switched on the radio. "The snow continues to fall," the radio announcer proclaimed. "We already have ten inches in Boston, over a foot of snow in the northern and western suburbs, and a foot and a half outside of Route 495. We'll have the school cancellations for you in two minutes but for now — we repeat — a snow emergency is in effect in the following cities: Boston, Brookline, Cambridge, Chelsea, Everett, Framingham, Revere, Somerville and Watertown. If you don't need to travel today, please stay home. The MTA reports that trains are running on schedule but the Green Line is experiencing delays above ground. Many buses are unable to complete their routes and the city has set up a special hotline for people concerned with specific routes. Call 423-8787 for specific transit information."

I lay back in my bed, wrapping the blankets tightly around myself, snuggling under the covers. School had to be called off, I thought to myself. There's no way there'll be school with a foot of snow on the ground. The buses will never get up Shawmut Hill.

I knew that I wouldn't be able to get back to sleep until I heard the definitive word that school was cancelled. Usually we began our faculty telephone chain at about 6:30, but I couldn't wait until then. I hoped that Miss Clarkson had phoned the radio stations already.

The announcer began to blare the school closings. I was always amused at the delivery of these cancellations. Keeping the schools in alphabetical order led to a massive tongue twister which taxed the abilities of even the most articulate announcer. "No school today in Acton, Arlington, Ayer, Bedford, Bellingham, Belmont, Beverly, Boston, Boxboro, Boxford, Brookline, Burlington, Cambridge, Carlisle, Chatham, Chelmsford, Chelsea, Cohasset, Concord, Dartmouth ... "

I tuned the radio carefully to make sure that the static of my old transistor wouldn't prevent me from hearing the good news. I glanced out the window to the streetlights, standing like silent statues wearing top hats of snow. No plough had been through the back streets of Somerville and deep snow was drifting into roadblocks at the end of our driveway.

"Medford, Melrose, Middle Valley School, Milford, Milton, Montague, Natick, Newburyport, Newton, Newton Country Day, Needham, Norwell, Norwood . . . "

My mind raced as I anticipated the arrival of the "S's". Were there any schools that did not seem to be called off ? Had they mentioned Brookline? We usually had off when Lexington schools were cancelled and the Lexington schools had been announced. Would I attempt to go to school anyway, even in the snow, if Clarkson refused to call off school?

"Raleigh Prep, Raynham, Rehoboth, Salem, Seekonk, Shawmut Hills School . . . "

I heaved a sigh of relief, shut off the radio, pulled the blankets over my head, and settled back into sleep.

I was awakened at 9:30 by a knock on my door. Pulling the blankets off my head, I muttered a groggy, "Come in," and squinted in the sunlight. The door pushed open and in came Holly, carrying a mug of cocoa and wearing her flannel nightie and furry slippers.

"No school today for us teachers, huh?" she said. "You got a call at seven from Alice, but I told her that you were asleep and she said that she'd take care of your calls on the phone chain. I heard you up and about at five, listening to the radio but I wasn't sure if you'd gone back to bed when Alice called."

"Were you up at that time?" I asked in surprise.

"Am I a schoolteacher?" Holly shot back. "Come on. After the snow predictions last night, I'll bet there wasn't a teacher in New England who wasn't up at dawn listening to the school closings."

I took a sip of the cocoa. "Who else is home?" I asked.

"Everyone," Holly answered. "There's no way anyone in Somerville is going anywhere and it's still snowing. Two of our roommates are downstairs making french toast, and the rest of the gang is being adventurous and attempting to walk to the 24-hour store to see if they have any milk. It's really beautiful outside because the ploughs haven't been through and it's still snowing and the winds are whipping things up. Putnam Street looks like a tub of vanilla ice cream."

"Are you glad there's no school today?" I asked.

"What are you, crazy?" she answered. "Of course I'm glad. I just hope it stops snowing soon, because we can't take much more and those winds are terrible. There must be a foot and a half out there already and the drifts are six feet high. *Somebody* in this house is going to have to shovel."

Just then the doorbell rang. "I'll get it," Holly said, and bounded down the stairs that led from my room. I pulled myself out of bed, put on my bathrobe and slippers, and trudged down the back stairway to the kitchen.

As I poured myself a cup of cocoa, the kitchen door swung open and Holly walked in, leading a snow-covered figure in a big, bright blue parka, encrusted with snow. As the hood was untied, the scarf pulled off, and the parka unzipped, snow and ice flew in all directions. Finally, a human being emerged — red-nosed, twinkle-eyed, Paul.

"What are you doing here?" I asked in amazement. "And how did you get here? The streets aren't ploughed yet?"

Paul blew his nose on a napkin, wiped it, and blew it again. Holly shoved a cup of hot chocolate in his hand and he took a large drink. He wiped the snow off his beard with the napkin, took another gulp, and then said, "I went for a walk after I'd heard that my school was called off, and I guess I kept walking." His eyes lit up and grew wide. "It's so beautiful out there," he said in amazement. "You should see Union Square. It's covered with snow, without a car in sight, and there's smoke coming up from the chimney in the fire station. It makes Somerville look like a little New England village."

"Are any stores open?" I asked.

"Only in Cambridge. I didn't see anything open once I hit Somerville. Even Dunkin' Donuts."

A plate of eggs and tofu was thrown onto the table, along with two forks. "I already ate," said Holly. "You boys fight over the food."

As Paul and I dug into the food, he looked up at me. "So what are you doing today?" he asked.

"I guess we're shoveling snow and hanging out," I responded. "Were you planning on walking back to Cambridge?"

Paul glanced out the window. "I don't think I could even if I wanted to," he answered. "You've got company for the day . . . and you folks may have to put me up for the night, as well."

Holly, Paul and I sat inside and watched the snow falling through most of the day. Two of my roommates attempted to shovel snow on several occasions, but the winds continued to whip it back into place. We played cards, baked bread, and watched television news reports of the storm damage. By dinnertime, the snow had cast eight-foot drifts throughout Putnam Street, school closings had already been announced for the following day, and the storm had been dubbed the Blizzard of '78. After a dinner of stir-fried vegetables and rice, Paul and Holly came up to my room and we huddled under blankets, swapping teacher stories.

"I was offered a contract for next year right before we left for vacation," Paul said, "but I'm not sure I'm going to accept it."

"What's the problem?" Holly asked.

"There are all kinds of crazy things going on at the school. We're supposed to be a progressive school for special needs students, but the director of the school has been acting strange lately," he explained. "She's been doing scary things to the kids and being very inconsistent with the staff. She's doing all she can to prevent the faculty from forming a union."

Holly interrupted. "We don't receive our contracts for a few more months," she said, "but I have some doubts too about whether I want to return to South Boston High School. After two years of trying to work in coalition with other teachers of all races as a positive force in this racist school system, I'm exhausted, and I don't get any sense of commitment from the School Committee or from the headmaster and administration of my school. The struggle is exhausting and takes my energy away from my students."

"Well, I guess I'm in the same position as both of you," I said cautiously, "because I'm not sure what I should do about returning to Shawmut Hills. My gripes are not the same as yours. Despite the humiliatingly low salary, I love my students and I love the teaching I'm doing. I also feel very warmly towards the school and the town, despite the pompous suburban airs it likes to take on."

"Then what's the problem?" Paul asked, propping a pillow behind his head.

I thought for a moment about how to express my conflict in words. "I have become increasingly aware of the conflict I feel between being a politically active person and being a schoolteacher in a conservative private school. As you both know, I've been slowly coming out of the closet in most of my life, but I still have to keep things secret at school. This means that I do my writing for the gay press under a pseudonym, I avoid being in photographs at gay events, and I sometimes lie to people at school about my personal life."

"Eric, these are just some of the sacrifices teachers have to make these days," Holly said. "I mean, I can't let my students know about most of my political views and the work I do fighting for the integration of the schools has to be kept outside the classroom."

"The tensions are different for me, Holly," I said, trying to put into the words the feelings I'd been struggling with for many months. "For me to feel good about who I am — as a person, including as a gay man — I have to be able to get rid of these vestiges of lying about myself. On some level it hurts me everytime I have to disguise my identity to do gay political work. I don't think I'll be able to feel like a fully integrated person until I'm out of the closet in all parts of my life."

"From what you've told me," Paul said, "that's going to mean leaving Shawmut Hills. I don't know of any teachers in this part of the world who can be open about being gay — either in public or private school. I know a couple of teachers who are gay, but they never discuss it and, I'll tell you, at my school I think they'd lose their jobs if they came out."

I thought for a moment. "I guess what I'm looking for from the two of you is support to leave teaching. I love the work I'm doing and I guess I'm doing a decent job with the kids. But for my mental health, it's important for me to come out of the closet all the way. It's taking that step and leaving a career that will be difficult."

"What will you do for work?" Paul asked. "It's not that easy finding any kind of jobs these days."

I hadn't thought about that, and Paul's statement brought me into a direct confrontation with my aimless future. "I suppose I would look for a job as a writer, or some kind of political work, or just start waiting on tables."

"Think about it carefully, before you make any big decisions," Paul said with an element of caution in his voice. "You might feel it's best for you to come out all the way, but when you have to take on work to support yourself that isn't interesting or creative, you might have second thoughts."

Noticing that Holly hadn't said anything for a few minutes, Paul turned to her. "What do you think?"

"I was wondering whether what you're suggesting isn't a little defeatist for my tastes," she began. "I was thinking that it might be possible for you to be open about everything *and* continue to teach at the school. I haven't heard of any openly gay teachers in this part of the country and I do know that some teachers have been fired once they've been found out, but I wonder whether it might not be possible, if you plan it right, to keep your job and still be open about things."

I thought for a moment about what she was saying. It seemed amazing to even consider the possibility, but I wanted to hear more.

Holly continued. "Perhaps you should think about it for a

few more weeks until you get your contract. Then it might be a good idea to return the contract with a little note letting the school know that you'd love to return, and they should know that you're gay, political, and you're going to be open about it. That would leave the ball in their court.

"I think you shouldn't assume the worst, although I agree you've got to be prepared as it might happen. Good teachers are rare these days and I think schools are beginning to recognize that fact. Shawmut Hills might not want to lose you and might be willing to change their ways a little to allow for your activism."

"So what you're suggesting, Holly, is that I go through the whole process of coming out at the school and see if they'd allow me to continue?" I asked.

"Yes. Instead of getting caught in the act, or having someone expose you at school, you should give them the information and see what they do with it."

"Things could get pretty wild," Paul said, a look of concern and doubt coming over his face. "You'd have to be prepared for some hostile reactions from other teachers, and you'd have to be ready to do a lot of public education."

"That's right," Holly said. "You would need all the patience in the world, because people are going to react in ways you can't imagine right now and if I know you, you're going to consider it your responsibility to help them work through their feelings. This is what educating the public is all about, but I'll tell you: As someone who does a lot of this kind of thing, it isn't a lot of fun and it zaps all your energy."

"I've got a couple of weeks to think about all of this," I said tentatively. "Right now, it sounds as if you've suggested to me a compromise between leaving silently and remaining at Shawmut Hills while keeping things in the closet. It sounds like an idea I could live with, but I think that the work involved in the process would really tax my patience." Then, smiling at my two friends, I continued. "And as you both know, patience is not my strong suit."

"No, it's not," Paul said, "and everyone knows that. But you can count on us, I'm sure, if you decide to take this path. We'll be there every step of the way."

Holly agreed. "Yes, we will. So don't feel as if you have to make any final decisions now. Think for a few weeks and we'll talk about it some more." She got up and walked to the window. "And it's still snowing, she said. "If this keeps up, we won't be back in school before springtime and you may not have to make your decision for months."

On February first, each teacher at Shawmut Hills School knew he or she would have individual meetings with Miss Clarkson. We expected to receive our formal offers of contracts for the coming year on that day. We had received notes during the previous week with the time of our meetings which sent us all into corners, discussing with great anticipation what our raises would be for the coming year, whether or not we were planning to return, and what our demands would be should we have the kindness to deign to return to this humble institution of learning. Teachers seemed to be at their most rebellious during this part of the year and, by the time contracts were due back, a month later, most teachers seemed to have vented their gripes and were happy to return.

When I walked into Miss Clarkson's office that day, she rose from her chair and greeted me with a warm smile and a handshake. We sat and she began her talk, glancing only occasionally at her prepared notes.

"You know, Eric, how very pleased we all are with your work at the school. Your creativity and enthusiasm are very gratifying to observe and we very much hope that you are planning to return to Shawmut Hills for a third year." Clarkson paused here and looked at me with a sincere look on her face. "I am aware that you and I have not always seen eye to eye on many aspects of the school. Your choices of Christmas plays, for example, go against my very concept of how we should observe the holidays in this school. De-emphasizing religion gives me great concern for these children. But I hope you realize that I very much respect your

ideas and appreciate the work you've done on our school committees. I have been impressed with your strong commitment to
your students and to our school."

I kept my mouth shut and allowed her to continue. "We're
prepared to offer you a significant raise over the next year, and
we're also hoping that you will continue to serve on the school's
Curriculum Committee. I know that the entire board of the
school joins me in hoping that you'll return."

I thanked Miss Clarkson and told her that I'd consider the
offer. Before I turned to leave, she handed me an envelope, in
which, I assumed, was a contract.

"This is due back on March 15," she said, "but as soon as you
make your decision, we'd appreciate hearing from you. We like to
let parents know that the teachers are continuing. This allows
them to fill in their own contracts for next year with confidence."

Before I left the room, I turned to Miss Clarkson. "I've got a
lot to think over," I said, holding up the envelope. "I promise that
you'll be the first to know, once my decision is made."

I spent the next two weeks agonizing over the decision and talking regularly with Holly and Paul. My priest friend was no help —
he discouraged me from any openly gay political work and told
me I was crazy to consider coming out to the head of my school. I
alternately decided he was right about returning and keeping
things quiet for another year, and rebelled against him, determined to return and shoulder the burden that I expected my coming out to cause. During the moments of my deepest conflict, it
was easy to choose the path of least resistance — leaving Shawmut Hills without saying anything about being gay — but these
periods didn't last long and I'd again find myself torn between the
other possibilities.

A day before contracts were due, I again came to the conclusion that I had reached during my snowbound discussions with
Holly and Paul. I would return a signed contract along with a letter politely informing Miss Clarkson that I was gay. It would be
short and to the point. I'd send it to her so that it would arrive at

her home on a Saturday. That would give her a day to think things over — and a weekend for me to worry myself frantic.

On a chilly Thursday night in early March, I sat down and composed the following letter:

Dear Miss Clarkson,

You will find my contract enclosed, signed and returned to you. I would be very happy to return for a third year at Shawmut Hills School. As we discussed in our meeting on February 1st, I feel it is important for both the stability of the school and the stability of my career.

There is another factor that I have had to weigh heavily in my mind before making my decision. I have not shared this with you until this point because I have felt that it does not affect my teaching and it has not come up at school. However, due to certain circumstances which I have considered at length, it is important for you to know now that I am gay. It has not been important for you to know this until this point because although I am an activist and a writer, I have avoided publicity due to my uncertainty as to how you would react. My writing has been under a pen name. This has made for a relatively comfortable way for me to be both a teacher and a gay person simultaneously.

The situation has changed and it is no longer comfortable for me. I have become increasingly concerned, over these past few months, of being "found out" — of having you, or anyone connected with the school, discover that I am gay. I believe that I am a good teacher, and your offering me a contract indicates that you feel similarly. Yet I am uncertain as to what your reaction to this disclosure will be. In any case, I cannot continue with the fear, and since I have always tried to be honest and direct with you, I am relating this information.

For several reasons, I have decided that I am going to write under my real name in the future. I write for both the local and national gay press, and I am certain that someone from the school will notice my by-line. The *Boston Globe* is considering an article I've written and it is written on a gay theme under my real name. If the article is published over the summer, and someone approaches you with the information, I would not want you to be shocked or surprised.

I have written this letter so that you will have time to think over its content before we meet. It is a difficult subject for me to confront you with directly, since I have no idea how you will react. I would like to get together as soon as possible and discuss the ramifications of this letter. I would greatly appreciate it if you would hold this letter in confidence until we talk.

Sincerely,
Eric E. Rofes

I read the letter several times, pondering whether there were not better ways to deliver my messge. Was I too strident? Not strident enough? Should I have been briefer? Should I have provided more explicit details?

I knew I'd have to drop the letter in the mailbox that evening, or I'd never get to sleep. I brought the letter into Holly's room, wanting her official endorsement before heading to the corner mailbox.

She read the letter carefully and then looked up at me. "You're really going to send her this letter, aren't you?" she said softly. "I am amazed at the courage you have. I just want you to know that, no matter what happens, I'll stand beside you and support you through the process."

I hugged Holly close to me. "I can't believe I'm going to send this letter," I said. "But it's the only way for me. I couldn't just leave and not raise the issue. I've got too much spunk in me and I've never learned how to back down from a fight."

That was the longest weekend of my life. I imagined Miss Clarkson receiving the letter on Saturday afternoon, fetching her mail from her house's mailbox, placing the pile before her on her oak dining table, and sorting through the letters, magazines and packages. She would note the return address and wonder what I had sent her. Then I envisioned her reaching for a gold inlaid envelope opener, carefully slitting the envelope open, and delicately removing the letter from inside.

She'd pull her glasses up by the eyeglass chain around her neck and quickly scan the letter. Then she'd read it, slowly — sentence by sentence — until she reached the line where I stated "It is important for you to know that I am gay."

That's when she'd drop dead — right there — clutching the letter to her breast, falling over from the chair, her head hitting the oak table, then her body slumping limply onto the floor. She'd be found later that day by the cleaning lady — cold, blue, with my crumpled letter in her hand.

Or perhaps that wouldn't happen at all. Instead she'd gasp at that line, rise from the chair, and, incredulous as she read the rest of the letter, begin screaming, her voice filled with horror. She'd rip the letter to shreds, rush to the phone, call the president of the school's board of trustees and call an emergency meeting that evening to demand my immediate dismissal. By the time I'd arrive at school on Monday morning, a posse of suburban station wagons would be waiting for me at the crest of the hill, filled with armed mothers pointing their rifles out their car windows while a pack of my students lined the road, pelting the disgraced teacher with snowballs.

Throughout the weekend, my mind continuously replayed different scenarios. Would she call me to discuss the letter or would she read it calmly, put it out of her mind, and go to the theater with a friend as if nothing happened? It is impossible to predict the personal reaction of a person whom one has never seen fully as a person. Perhaps, I decided, it was best to put these thoughts from my mind, and summon up all my strength to get myself to school on Monday.

7

On Monday morning I arrived at school at eight o'clock, my usual time. The schoolyard looked no different, and there were no police cars anticipating my arrival. I entered the office, signed in on the daily record sheet, and cast a quick glance at my mailbox hoping to find a note from Miss Clarkson. As I removed the jumble of mimeographed notices and memos, I heard a door open, and turned to find myself facing the headmistress.

"Good morning, Eric," she said in that familiar, crisp morning voice.

"Good morning, Miss Clarkson," I responded.

"We've gotten a call from Arthur's mother. He's come down with the flu over the weekend and won't be in today. Scott is also sick with a cold," she informed me. "Also, Zayna is ill so your class won't be having Drama today. Please adjust your schedule accordingly."

I nodded agreeably as I fumbled to stuff the memos from my mailbox into my backpack. Was that it? I wondered. Did the letter arrive? Had I actually ever sent it? Or was this all a bad dream? My mind began to race frantically.

Miss Clarkson turned to return to her office, but as she approached the door, she turned again. "Oh, by the way, Eric. I'd like to meet with you second period, if that's convenient."

I glanced nervously at my schedule book. Second period was free. "Fine," I said. "I'll come down right after nine o'clock."

"That will be fine," she said, a slight smile pursing her lips. "I'll see you then."

The next hour passed slowly. I guided my class through the spelling and vocabulary words for the week but my mind was on other matters. After class, as the children rushed off to their math teacher, I composed myself, pushed in my chair, and attempted to stroll calmly to the office. I took a short-cut through the library and passed Alice, her head buried in the card catalog.

"Good morning, Eric," she said, looking at me through her eyeglasses like an owl. "I hope you've had a nice restful weekend."

I thought for a minute to myself. It was now or never to tell Alice. I looked around the library and no one was in sight. "Do you have a second to chat, Alice?" I asked.

Sensing the serious tone of my voice, Alice immediately slid the catalog drawer into its cabinet and beckoned me to her desk. "What's on your mind, friend?" she said with a smile.

I took a deep breath. "I'd rather you hear it from me, Alice, than from anyone else. I might not be returning to Shawmut Hills next year."

Alice's poker face took on a decidedly troubled demeanor. "Why's that, if I may ask?"

"I sent Clarkson a note this weekend telling her that I'm gay and telling her that I do political work for gay rights. I have an appointment to talk with her about it in two minutes." I glanced nervously at the clock on the wall.

A smile came over Alice's face. "You do have chutzpah, don't you Eric?"

"Either that or I'm crazy."

"I would've liked to have seen Beatrice's face when she opened your note. She must've dropped dead."

"I guess I'll find that out in a few minutes. I'm just as concerned with how the other teachers take this news as with what Clarkson's reaction is."

"Well, don't worry about me, Eric. I've known for a while. I've known about my kid brother and I just sort of assumed you were gay as well. It doesn't make a bit of difference to me. A good teacher is a good teacher. We need you in this school, regardless of your sex life."

"Do you have any idea what reaction I'll be getting out of the front office?"

"No, but I wish I could be a fly on the wall. I've never known Beatrice to have to deal with anything of this nature. I expect she'll rise to the occasion, as always, but I'm sure it won't be easy."

I moved toward the exit door. Alice called to me before I left the room "Good luck, kid," she said. "I know you'll be nervous in there, but try to keep your wits about you. I want to hear *everything* she says."

On entering Miss Clarkson's office, I took the seat offered to me and gazed around the room at the various plants and turtle knick-knacks on display. Never before had the place seemed so intimidating to me. Miss Clarkson arose from her seat, shut the door, and began speaking to me.

"As you might have guessed, I received your letter this weekend. I was — how shall we put it — surprised by your message." She paused here and looked me directly in the eye. "I must thank you for giving me a day or two to think things over. Needless to say, it's not every day that I've had to consider such matters. I really am still at a loss regarding what to do. I hope that you won't mind me asking you a few questions, before we decide how to proceed."

"That's fine," I said in a quiet voice, my feet planted firmly beneath my chair.

"First of all," she said, "And you must forgive my ignorance, but is this all something new for you or have you been . . . this way . . . for a while?"

Educating the public again, just as Holly had predicted. "Some of the political activism is new for me," I answered, "but as far as being gay goes, that has been true for me for quite some time."

She glanced down at a piece of paper, and I realized that she had prepared a list of questions for me. "When you say that you write for the local and national gay press, what do you mean? Are there magazines that you read that are different from the magazines I know about?"

"Most major cities have newspapers and magazines that provide the local gay community with information and news. In Boston, we have a paper called the *Gay Community News*, for which I write. There are also national newspapers, magazines, newsletters."

Miss Clarkson appeared perplexed. "What I don't understand, is what is different or unique about these newspapers? How are they different from the *Boston Globe*?"

"Generally, they tend to come out less frequently," I explained, noting my pun with a quick chuckle to myself, "and they tend to focus on news about gay rights organizing or gay social groups — events and happenings within the gay community." From the expression on Miss Clarkson's face, I could tell that she still was not getting the message. I took a different approach.

"You see, what might be confusing to you, is that you might not realize there is a whole community out there made up of men and women who participate in social and political gay organizations. As much as we all have our jobs, personal backgrounds, and family situations, many gay people have formed a community together for support and —" I stopped short. "It's really hard to explain," I said, feeling frustrated by my inadequate attempt.

"What kind of groups are you involved with?"

"In addition to the newspaper, I'm also involved in a Gay Men's Center—"

"What's that?" she interrupted.

"It's a resource center that's sort of a gathering place for gay men in Boston. I also work with a group called Committee for

Gay Youth that provides support for teenagers who are gay."

This seemed to strike her interest. "Are there really teenagers who are that way? I really hadn't imagined that."

"Some teenagers are already aware that they're gay. Others seem kind of confused about it. We're finding more and more adolescents who tell their parents that they're gay and are kicked out of the house. They end up on the streets of Boston and Committee for Gay Youth attempts to make sure that streetworkers and social service agencies are able to help these kids."

"Most of them must be from poorer families. I can't imagine teenagers getting thrown out onto the streets in this community."

"As a matter of fact," I added, "many of the kids *are* from 'respectable' suburban homes. I only know of two kids from Shawmut Hills, but many are from places like Newton, Lexington, Lincoln, Concord, all around here."

"Tell me, do teenagers who think that they're homogenized — I mean homosexual — ever grow up to be heterosexual?"

I kept myself from smiling at her slip, but made a mental note to remember the error for the rest of my life. "Some of the kids in the group come in with fairly confused ideas about their sexual orientation, and the program has a strict policy of being non-judgmental, and accepting a kid's being gay or straight or whatever. So I guess all I can say is that some kids who think they're gay don't turn out to be gay, while some kids who think they're straight also don't turn out to be straight."

Miss Clarkson glanced out the window, thinking about this for a moment. Then she looked down at her list of questions and shifted the focus for a bit.

"How do you think this information would affect your relationship with the children?" she asked.

I was prepared for this question. "I think that the news will be surprising for them," I began, "but I don't think it needs to be confusing or difficult. There are many openly gay teachers now teaching in many parts of the country, and in general they seem to be able to explain this information, deal with the problems that might arise, and put it behind them to continue their teaching. I think some of the children will be upset, but for most of them, I don't think it'll make a difference. Their parents probably will have more concerns than they do," I added.

"Ah, yes," she agreed. "I was wondering what parental reaction would be. I wonder whether parents will take their children out of the school, or avoid sending their children here in the first place, or if there will be a lot of publicity about this."

"I can't anticipate what will happen with this parent body. My sense is that most of the parents seem to feel very positively about my program, and I'd bet that that's more important to them than the fact that I'm gay."

"I'm not sure I agree with you," Miss Clarkson said, "But that's clearly something we won't know for a while, will we? Tell me, have you discussed this matter with other teachers in the school?"

I immediately wondered what was at the root of the question, but answered anyway. "No, not yet," I fibbed. "I'm hoping to talk to some of my friends about it during the week, but I wanted to hear your thoughts before I opened up the subject with anyone. I'll probably be talking with Zayna and Alice, and maybe Marie," I said.

There was pause here. I found myself realizing that, despite the discussion we'd just had, I still didn't have any idea what Miss Clarkson was thinking. "I've appreciated your questions, Miss Clarkson, but I'm left wondering what you think of all of this."

She looked directly at me and thought for a moment. She pursed her lips, turned and looked out the window, and then turned back to me. "To be totally honest with you, Eric, I really don't know what to say. I am really uncertain as to how to react to this information and I will be seeking help from Doug Cabot, the president of the school's board of trustees. I think that, before any decisions are made, or before this information comes out, we'd better all sit down and have a discussion."

I bristled at this suggestion. Doug Cabot was a conservative, stodgy sort of guy. I didn't know him well and I had managed to keep my distance from him throughout my time at Shawmut Hills. As president of the school board, he was an intimidating presence to many teachers, as he controlled the school's finances and educational policy. He was blamed by some of the progressive faculty members for taking a middle-of-the-road school and steering it into a traditional prep school image, yet he was universally respected as a man of sound judgment and vision. Another factor causing me concern was that Cabot's daughter was in the fifth grade and would be in my class should I remain in the school.

"Well," Miss Clarkson said rising from her seat. "I have no more questions. I have found this discussion to be — how should we say — very informative, and I appreciate your willingness to explain these matters to me."

"I've also appreciated this meeting," I said in my most diplomatic voice. "Let me know when we'll be meeting with Mr. Cabot."

Miss Clarkson extended her hand to me. As I shook it, she said to me with a smile, "I must say that you constantly surprise me, Eric."

I returned the smile, turned, and quickly left the room.

That evening, I received a phone call from Paul. "Did you do it?" he asked. I could sense the excitement in his voice.

"Yes, I did. Clarkson got the letter and we had a meeting about it today."

"What happened? What did she say?"

"Well, one thing she did was confuse the word 'homogenized' for 'homosexual.' I could have died."

"I hope you corrected her politely and controlled your laughter."

"I did my best."

"So what did she think about you being gay and all that?"

"Well, she really didn't know what to think. I guess she's pretty confused about the whole thing. The librarian told me that Clarkson's never had to deal with this kind of thing before."

"Did you come out to the librarian, too?"

"I had to, Paul. I needed some support within the school."

"I guess I could understand that. So, tell me what happened. Did you get fired?"

"It's not that easy. I'm going to have to meet with the president of the school board this week and talk about it with him. He's a fairly intimidating Brahmin type, but I think he's pretty sensible."

"How long do you expect this will be kept under wraps? I'm sure the parents and the kids will find out soon."

"I hope not," I answered. "I've got more than I can deal with at this point, all I need is my phone ringing off the hook from parents worried about the queer teaching their little kids."

"How are you feeling about all this now?"

I paused for a moment. How *was* I feeling? In the rush of the day, with all the madness of teaching and dealing with Clarkson and grading exams and holding several parent conferences, I hadn't taken the time to notice how I felt.

"Scared shitless, Paul," I confessed, feeling the fear pulse through my body. "Scared absolutely shitless."

The next week passed by in a rush of hushed encounters as word somehow mysteriously leaked out into the school community about my situation. I found myself fecklessly attempting to defend my reasons for raising the issue while also trying to find support and comfort among sympathetic faculty members. I deliberately met with some key colleagues to tell them what was happening and I was pleased and surprised by their responses.

Zayna, the drama and art teacher for the school, seemed awestruck by what I was doing. As I sat with her in her studio sipping tea, she looked at me wide-eyed and exclaimed, "I just can't believe you were sitting there talking to Beatrice about anything that has to do with sexuality or your personal life. This is all so foreign to her. She must be climbing the wall with this situation."

"I felt this was the best way to go about the matter," I responded. "Otherwise, I would just have had to leave teaching without putting up a fuss and maybe — just maybe — this'll all turn out for the better and I'll be allowed to stay at Shawmut Hills."

Zayna looked at me with doubt in her eye. "I know what the board of this school is like and, I can tell you, they don't want any teacher in this school who is going to cause controversy. I admire you for what you're doing, Eric, but I'm afraid I'm not very optimistic.

"One thing's for sure, though. I want you to know that you can count on me for support — both personally and within the faculty. If you need me to lobby anyone or take a public stand, I will be glad to speak on your behalf."

I was touched by the offer. "Thanks, a lot," I said. "That means a lot to me."

Other teachers presented more difficult situations. The girls' gym teacher, who had recently become engaged to her high-school sweetheart, tried her best to be supportive but clearly struggled with the issue.

One morning, while I was alone in the faculty room, she entered and raised her questions.

"Now, Eric," she said in a voice that I knew would be lecturing me in a covert manner. "I want you to know that I think the school should keep you, even if you are a homosexual. But what I don't understand is why you had to bring this whole thing up? I mean, no one would have guessed. I mean you're not one of those guys who you can tell right away is swishy and stuff like that. I mean, I had my suspicions about you. I even once asked Marie if she thought you were gay — mainly because you seemed to have few girlfriends around and I noticed a couple times that you seemed to have more interest in guys than girls. But, I mean, you're a good teacher and you had a bright future ahead of you. Why'd you have to bring up all your dirty laundry?"

Again I thought about what Holly had told me about patience and educating the public, and the kinds of drivel with which I'd have to deal. I took a deep breath. "Well, I don't consider it dirty. I don't even consider it laundry. But I felt that I needed to be more open about my political work on gay issues, if I'm going to continue to teach here."

She looked at me and chose another line of reasoning. "Well, what do your parents think about all this? I mean, I have Jewish parents too and I know how protective they can be. I mean, aren't they all upset about you telling everyone about your private life?"

"My parents really have nothing to do with this." I answered. "I've told them what's going on and I bet they think I'm crazy on one hand, and they respect me on the other hand. But they're three hundred miles away on Long Island, and they're not very involved in my life at this point."

The faculty room door creaked open and in walked Chuck Ritter, basketball under his arm, whistle dangling from his neck. He saw us talking, hesitated a moment, and then came in anyway, sheepishly. I could tell he felt awkward as he poured himself some coffee and took a seat. We greeted him and continued our talk.

The girls' gym teacher immediately drew Chuck into the conversation. "Chuck and I were talking about your situation today and we really do want to find a way to support you."

"Yeah," Chuck said. "I mean, I just don't think it's any of the school's business if you're gay or if I'm going out with three different girls at once or if some teacher gets pregnant. I just don't think these are good reasons for firing teachers. We ought to have a union here to make sure that these kinds of things don't happen at Shawmut Hills."

"Thanks for your support," I said to Chuck. "I guess I wondered how you'd react."

"Hey, man," he said defensively, "I've been to college. I had a friend at school tell me that he was gay and I saw the way he was treated by the guys in his frat house. He was really a decent guy, too. I just think everyone makes too big a deal about this kind of thing. It's nobody's business."

Then he stopped for a second and appeared to be lost in thought. A smile came over his face and he continued. "But, you, know, I'd have paid a million dollars to be in the room when Clarkson got that letter you sent her. She must've shit a brick."

I found a note in my box one morning that week from Jane Stebbins, the director of recruitment and admissions for the school and a woman who seemed as far different from me as anyone in the school. While we'd never become close friends, we had a cautiously supportive relationship. As Alice had once explained, we were natural allies because she was pleased with my teaching and knew that a strong sixth grade teacher was a good draw for the school's recruiting efforts. She also had a son who was entering the sixth grade and she very much wanted the boy to have a firm yet sensitive teacher. I knew that Jane supported my teaching and had the influence with the school administration to smooth over some of my rougher edges.

I came to Jane's office at the start of my lunch hour. She greeted me warmly, offered me a seat, then closed the office door.

This was the room that prospective parents sat in as they heard about the wonders of Shawmut Hills. On the walls were displayed bright paintings by kindergarten children, mounted essays by fifth graders, and colorful photographs by a professional photographer of happy children doing their schoolwork. I tried to imagine the impression this room gave to the as yet uninitiated.

Jane sat at her desk and looked at me intensely. "Before we go to lunch," she began, "I just wanted a second to chat with you in private. Last night, Dan and I talked about your, er, situation. You know how much we both admire your teaching and feel that you would be an excellent teacher for our son next year. We very much feel caught in the middle of this situation.

"Our church generally takes a pretty conservative view of homosexuality, and we've become very involved in the church during the past few years as the children have gotten older. I have to admit that I have a difficult time understanding why you are doing what you're doing. It seems to me that you're causing a lot of people to look at some difficult and controver-

sial issues that they'd never looked at before. You're also making my job a little difficult, because we've already accepted
several new families for your class next year, and they've
observed your teaching and are excited about having their
children with you."

Jane paused for a second and I noticed her purse her lips.
I was struck by the similarity in style between this attractive
young woman and Miss Clarkson. Jane was certainly more
humane and warmer than Miss Clarkson, but the two shared a
kind of professionalism that was formal, controlled, and ex-
ceedingly rational. There wasn't much room for emotions or
feelings in either of their styles.

"Dan and I would very much like to see you come back
next year, even with this bit of information about your personal
life," she said. "You know that Dan is friends with Doug Cabot,
the president of the school board. The two of them are having
lunch today and Dan has promised to put in a word for you. We
think that you're an asset to the school and to our child, and
we'd be sad to see you have to leave."

She reached for her handbag and, before giving me any time
to respond, said simply, "Now, let's go grab a sandwich and forget
this mess."

As it turned out, the meeting with Doug Cabot was not as
difficult as I had anticipated. Cabot seemed to be a reasonable,
if conservative, gentleman who expressed appreciation for the
way in which I was handling the matter. At the same time, he
was concerned about whether I intended to pursue legal re-
course should the school fire me.

I avoided answering some of his more pointed questions,
and he assured me that he would not be the sole party making
this major decision concerning my fate. It was entirely too
serious a matter to be left to Miss Clarkson and Mr. Cabot, he
told me. They would need to consult with the rest of the board
of directors of the school. Thus I found myself invited to attend

a special meeting of the board the following week. There I was told to expect to meet the trustees, answer their questions and, ultimately, meet my judgment.

8

I stood waiting by the front door for Alice and Marie to arrive and escort me to the board meeting. Aware that I'd be a wreck inside despite a composed public appearance, I had arranged to have friends accompany me this evening. Alice served as the faculty representative to the board, so she was expected to attend in any case. Marie had been granted special permission to be present at the meeting and lend silent support to her friend on trial. Thus I stood at the door, gazing out at dusk settling onto the streets of Somerville, waiting for my ride to Shawmut Hills, feeling like a convict about to walk his final mile.

Holly came bounding down the stairway with her hand behind her back. Arriving at the front door, she drew out a small bouquet of spring flowers and pressed it into my hand. "Here, honey," she said, smiling. "My best wishes go with you. I really wish I could be there to watch this performance. You'll do all of us proud, I'm sure."

I smelled the flowers and my spring allergies brought tears to my eyes. "Do I look all right?" I asked. "This is a difficult occasion to dress for. None of the fashion books give any indication of what to wear to an execution. I spent about an hour going through the closet and trying to decide what I could wear that would give me some degree of integrity, but not seem too blatant."

Holly looked me over from head to toe. "You look like the perfect preppie schoolteacher. The khakis, the oxford shirt and those loafers are strictly prepster. No one could challenge you tonight. The only thing that's missing is this," she said, reaching into her pocket and pulling out a metallic button which she pinned to my shirt. I looked down and saw the bright pink "Gay and Proud" button against my white shirt. Instinctively, I reached down to take it off, but Holly's hand caught mine.

"No," she said quietly. "Leave it on, at least till you arrive at school. It'll be comforting to know that it's there and you can be sure that — even in the madness of the night — you won't leave it on when you walk into the judge's chambers."

The phone rang and Holly rushed into the kitchen to answer it. I peered out the window, glanced nervously at my watch, and began to pace.

"It's for you," she called to me from the other room.

I directed my pacing toward the phone and grabbed it from Holly. "Hello?" I said, my voice cracking for the first time in years.

"It's just me, Eric." I heard Paul's voice at the other end of the line. "Just calling to send you best wishes for a pleasant evening on Firing Line."

"Thanks, I need all the support I can get."

"Remember, no matter what happens, you have the satisfaction of knowing you've handled this whole thing with a great deal of integrity."

"That's not going to keep me employed, Paul."

"No, it's not. And you might lose your job tonight, although I think they'd be crazy to let you go. But I think you've got to keep in mind that — no matter what happens — you've handled a difficult situation with a great deal of pride and dignity. This could have been a real mess for you and for the school. You've done the responsible thing."

I heard a car honking for me out front. "They're here!" I exclaimed. "I've got to go, Paul. Thanks for calling and call me at midnight and I'll let you know what happened!"

I dropped the phone onto the receiver, kissed Holly good-bye, grabbed my sweater and dashed down the walkway to the car.

The school library had always seemed to be one of the warmer, homier rooms of the school. Located in the center of the building and accessible to every classroom, it easily had become a reflection of Alice's personality over the last dozen years. Stacks of books and periodicals made it clear that this was a room that saw heavy use on a daily basis. The brightly colored finger paintings by first-grade children gave the room a down-to-earth feeling and the wood-stained panels added to the sense of formality and tradition that served to remind the viewer that this was — despite the warmth — an institution of learning.

Tonight as I entered the library, the formality of the wood-stained panels loomed large. The room took on a new feeling, a feeling of conservatism and seriousness. Only Miss Clarkson had arrived and she was carefully arranging the library chairs into a circle in the center of the room.

"Good evening," she said in an unusually awkward tone. "We're all a bit early for the meeting."

Alice and Marie took off their coats and tossed them onto one of the library tables. Plates of Fig Newtons sat on one of the desks, and a coffee machine was beginning to perk. I looked quickly around the room, wondering where I would be sitting when my final judgment was pronounced — by a jury that was distinctly *not* comprised of my peers.

Before I had a chance to ask, Miss Clarkson answered my question. "I think it's best for you to sit over there, Eric," she said, indicating a chair at the edge of the circle. "And Alice and Marie may sit wherever they'd like."

Marie came up beside me. "I'd like to sit next to you," she said, trying to sound cheery. "Is that okay?"

"It sure is," I responded.

"Are you sure you want to keep that button on all night?" she asked, indicating the pink button that I'd forgotten to remove.

I became flustered and took it off quickly, and we settled

into our seats just as the clock struck eight. The trustees slowly entered, one-by-one, and greeted us. Several of them were unfamiliar to me, and they introduced themselves and shook my hand. One of them — Peter Larkin — was the man responsible for connecting me to Shawmut Hills just two years earlier. He was one of my professors at Harvard, my thesis advisor, and a friend whom I'd never told about this side of my life. He greeted me and smiled in a way that seemed to express a shared sense of naughtiness — as if Peter and I had together sprung this controversy on the school. The smile was encouraging — the formality and seriousness of the other board members was beginning to feel unduly fatalistic.

When all twelve trustees had taken their seats, Doug Cabot began the meeting. "You all know why we're here tonight," he began, "and I thank you very much for arranging your schedules so that this meeting could take place on such short notice. I know that the last few weeks have been difficult for Eric, as they have been difficult for all of us who are in a situation that is unique and troublesome. As I've told all of you on the telephone, Eric, Miss Clarkson and I met last week and discussed a letter he'd written and enclosed with his contract for next year. In the letter, he explained that, not only is he gay, but he is a political activist and a writer. I think what we're here to discuss tonight is whether or not there is a future for Eric at Shawmut Hills knowing these additional pieces of information."

He paused here and I looked up from the floor where my eyes had been riveted since Mr. Cabot began to speak. I looked from one trustee to another. Serious faces all. One woman, a teacher of anthropology at a nearby high school, seemed troubled to the point of facial contortion. Her son Arthur had been my student during my first year in the school, and I always found her to be supportive and friendly. Her roles as a mother, board member and thinking person seemed to conflict in this situation.

Another trustee, a noted psychiatrist at Massachusetts General Hospital and the father of two young students at the school, seemed to be attempting to maintain a non-judgmental

look on his face. Showing no reaction to Doug Cabot's state-
ments, nor any semblance of emotion, he sat through the initial
statement with a studied, earnest look on his face.

My eyes glanced from one trustee to another. Only Alice was
able to shoot me an occasional smile or wink, and I worked to
control my own reaction.

"What I want to make clear from the start of this discussion,"
Cabot continued, "is that we're not here to judge Mr. Rofes as a
teacher. The offer of a contract for a third year at our school indicates that Miss Clarkson finds him to be a commendable teacher
and, indeed, most of us have heard very positive feedback from
parents and students since his arrival at the school. His ability to
challenge the students, as well as maintain strict discipline in the
classroom, are what we've wanted to have at the sixth grade level
for a long time. There is no doubt in my mind that we'd like to
keep Eric at the school and what this meeting is trying to determine is if it is possible for him to continue with us, despite these
recent revelations."

Cabot laid out the ground rules for the evening. It would be
strictly question and answer for an hour or so, and then I would
be asked to leave while the trustees discussed the matter and
voted on my continued presence in the school. I was to receive a
phone call from Cabot probably late that evening to inform me of
their decision.

The discussion began with a question from Doug Cabot.
"Why don't you tell us about how you arrived at the point where
you decided to send this letter to Miss Clarkson," he suggested.

This seemed like an innocuous starting point, I thought to
myself. "I sent the letter after two years of soul-searching," I
began. "During my first two years at the school, I have had a lot of
conflicting feelings about parts of my life. While I've been
developing my abilities to teach children and have been enjoying
my teaching experiences, I have also been feeling more and more
comfortable as a gay person. I've started to become involved in
gay community activities, including some political work. Thus
I've found myself torn between two lives that seem incompatible.

I'm trying to find a way to survive with them both as comfortably as possible."

"Have you deliberately kept these lives separate up until this point?" Cabot asked.

"Until now," I continued, "I was able to do my work as an activist under a pseudonym. I'd write articles under a fake name, stay out of pictures when the newspapers or television cameras covered an event in which I was involved, and I'd tell lies to people in the gay community about the work I did professionally.

"Even in this school, I'd allow parents and other staff members to attempt to set me up on blind dates with women, permit my students to have the impression that every woman I was seen with was my girlfriend, and I'd even find myself lying about my life to other teachers. I don't want to do these things anymore. I don't want to live with the lies and the deception and I don't want to feel split into two directions. I need to come clean with everyone and live an honest life."

I had spoken this speech in an unusually quiet tone of voice, attempting to keep my remarks free from the strident tones for which I had a tendency. While several trustees nodded, indicating their understanding of my predicament, others looked puzzled or disturbed. The psychiatrist was the only one eager to ask a question.

"Are there other teachers anywhere who are open about this kind of thing?" he asked. "If there are, I haven't heard about it."

"At this point, there are not any openly gay teachers in this part of the country below the college level," I answered. "However, in other parts of the country, teachers of young children, as well as junior high and high school teachers, are openly gay. In some cities teachers are actually protected in their contracts from losing their jobs because they're gay. There aren't hundreds of teachers who are open about this, but there are quite a few and most of them maintain that they simply address questions from their students when and if they come up and then they go about their teaching. It doesn't seem to have such a dramactic effect on the school or on their teaching as one would expect."

Arthur's mother had her hand raised and seemed to be troubled by something I'd said. "I guess what I'm most concerned with," she said, "are the ramifications of this matter for the children. I think all of us are aware of the possible influence this could have on the children's sexual orientation."

I was annoyed at this concern but I tried to keep my perspective. "What influence do you think this will have on the children?" I asked quietly.

"You are teaching children at a very formative age, Eric. Early adolescence is an important time for the kids. I'm concerned with the way this might influence them. Now, you have chosen to be this way yourself and that's your right and your business. But when you go public about it, you influence other people and this concerns me."

"Are you asking me if I think my talking to the children about my sexual orientation will influence them and encourage them to be gay?"

The woman thought for a moment. "I suppose that's what I'm afraid of. I've been told that you work with a group called Committtee for Gay Youth, and it seems to me that you're encouraging our young people to be this way. I'm not comfortable with that at all."

"I appreciate your expressing your concern," I said, attempting to appear in control of the matter while, in fact, I was enraged inside at the assumptions she was making. "Committee for Gay Youth does not encourage children or teenagers to have any particular sexual orientation."

Doug Cabot jumped in. "What does this group do, Eric?" he asked.

"We support kids when they choose to identify themselves as gay. We're not rigid at all and we support teens who evolve from one sexual orientation to another. While some adolescents seem to experience a great deal of confusion concerning their sexual orientations, I think it's important to acknowledge that some of them don't. We work primarily with those rare kids who are fifteen or sixteen years old and able to say to themselves 'I'm gay and I need to find some other kids like me.' Otherwise they would probably end up on the streets, without money, in some fairly desperate situations."

Arthur's mother wanted to pursue some points. "What you haven't answered in a way that satisfies me, is whether your coming out, as you call it, would influence our children later in life."

"Most of the studies I've read over the past few years seem to agree that sexual identity is formed during the first few years of life," I said, sounding like a schoolteacher. "By the time a child is in the sixth grade, his or her orientation is pretty well-formed. I think having a gay teacher would allow students who are gay to feel more comfortable with themselves, but I don't think it will cause students to have gay feelings if they wouldn't have had them otherwise."

"But what about these other students?" another woman asked quickly. I'd never before met her, but I knew that she was the director of a nearby hospital and the parent of a fourth-grade girl. She dressed conservatively and seemed a bit older than the other trustees. I had been warned that she might be hostile. "If your other students are primarily heterosexually oriented, in the normal fashion, shouldn't they be able to feel some support? If you tell them that you're homosexual, this might make them feel wrong or out of place."

"I'm sorry," I said, "but I feel there's already a lot of support within this school and within our society for kids who are heterosexual. From the wedding rings we see on teachers' fingers, to the ads we see on television, to most kids' parents, I feel that heterosexual teenagers receive a lot of support and validation."

I wasn't going to get off easy. She continued her hostile line of questioning. "I think this is clearly a question of values," she said in a serious tone. "The question for me is, do the parents of children at Shawmut Hills School want their children to be told that is okay to choose to be a homosexual? Because that's what we'd be doing if we condone this kind of activity on the part of our teachers."

I looked at Alice, needing a supportive face in my line of

vision at the moment. Alice was peering over her spectacles, staring with angry eyes at the woman, but she managed to sit quietly without letting her anger erupt. I decided to follow suit and let the bigotry speak for itself while I awaited the next rational question.

Doug Cabot sensed the tension in the room and changed the focus of the discussion. "I was wondering," he said, "whether it would be possible for you to continue doing your political work, as well as working with that youth project, and not let people know that you're a school teacher. You wouldn't necessarily have to tell people that you teach school, and I certainly think it would be fairly easy for you to keep the name of the school private. Would that be possible, Eric?"

While his suggestion was certainly possible, I wondered what he was getting at. If Cabot hoped to keep me at the school by having me hide my professional identity, it was a compromise that I could probably try to make. I told him so and then added, "I think it's highly unlikely that some people will not connect the gay activist Eric Rofes with the schoolteacher Eric Rofes. If I had a name like 'Doug Cabot', or any name more common than my own, I could see people not assuming they were the same person. But with my name, it seems likely that someone could connect the employee of this school to the activist quoted in the *Globe*.

It was my former professor, Peter Larkin's turn for a question. "What kinds of things can you foresee doing over the next year that would get your name into the *Boston Globe*?" he asked.

"I'm not sure that my name will end up in papers like that," I answered, "But it might. This summer and this fall I'll be doing some organizing work related to gay teachers, especially around the Briggs Initiative in California. That initiative is going to be on the ballot in November throughout the state of California, and would mandate that schools fire any employee who is supportive of gay rights. In my opinion, this is a very frightening thing and we've formed a committee here in Boston to do support work for the people organizing against it in California."

"What kind of work will you be doing?" Larkin continued.

"I'll be doing some public speaking on the issue, possibly as a gay schoolteacher. I don't think I have to announce where I teach school, but I think it's important for teachers around the country to speak out publicly against this initative."

"Do you mean to say that any schoolteacher in California who speaks positively about gays would be fired under this law?" The question came from a trustee I hadn't noticed before who was sitting in the back of the room, puffing on his pipe. "I find that incredible."

"Yes, it would cause such firings," I answered. "I think this helps you to realize why it's important for me to get involved. This kind of thing is pretty dangerous. Any teacher — gay or straight — who simply said it was okay for gays to have rights, could legally lose their jobs."

"If you were allowed to continue to teach here," interjected Doug Cabot, "how would you deal with the subject with the children? Would you allow the issue to come up in the classroom?"

"The subject comes up anyway," I said. "I'm afraid that many of you don't realize that, with sixth graders, at least, homosexuality comes up all the time. When I walked into the classroom two years ago, I vowed never to raise the subject. It came out of the kids all the time. Whether it's questions in health class, current event articles brought in about Anita Bryant, taunts on the playing field, or books in the classroom, homosexuality has found its way into the classroom. Any teacher could tell you that."

Alice spoke up. "What do you mean by books in the classroom?" she asked curiously.

I'd never talked with Alice about this, but I supposed now was as good a time as any for her to find out. "When I began teaching here, I took home copies of all the reading books we had for sixth graders in multiple copies. One of them is a wonderful book called *The Man Without A Face*, which has won all kinds of awards. It's a moving story about a boy from a troubled family and the man who befriends him and becomes his tutor.

"Well, the climax of the book involves the two of them sleeping together in quite an ambiguous manner that leaves the boy confused and disturbed. Now I've never had my students read the book, but I assume that if we have 22 copies of it in my classroom, some teacher has. I raise this issue only to let you know that whether or not I'm teaching this class, homosexuality is a subject that will be dealt with in one way or another. It was here before I got to this school, and it will be here long after I'm gone."

Doug Cabot still seemed concerned. "That is helpful for us to know, Eric, but you didn't answer my question. How would you discuss the matter with the children?"

I paused for a moment while I thought about my response. "I would have to do a little research before I talked to the kids about being gay. Just off the top of my head, I think I'd want to explain to them that I was gay and tell them what it meant. I'd make sure to explain it in more than sexual terms, since too often kids see relationships between adults purely in terms of sex. I'd explain that being gay means that my deepest feelings go toward other men. Then I'd ask them if they had any questions. It would probably be a good idea to break into smaller groups at this time and have the groups develop questions. Then we'd come back and hear their questions."

"What would you tell them about sex, if they asked about it?" the psychiatrist asked.

"I suppose I'd want to make sure that they realized that sex was more than just genital contact, that it involved hugging and kissing and touching."

"Then you'd answer their questions about sex," he continued increduously.

I knew it was the wrong thing to say but I took a deep breath, glanced at Marie, and answered, "Yes. I believe that children's questions about sex should be answered honestly."

I think it was at this point that several of the trustees made up their mind that I was a lost cause. Both the psychiatrist and the hospital director grew silent for the next forty minutes while the other trustees shifted into discussions about homosexuality and children which ranged from discussing the stereotypes about child molestation to the current far-fetched sociobiological theory that nature created homosexuals to care for children of other people while the parents were busy reaping harvests or killing dinosaurs. I was asked quite personal questions about when I'd come out, my relationship with my parents, and whether or not I had a "partner."

I felt many of the trustees were sincerely struggling to grasp the issues and I was pleased with the range of questions asked. I had a difficult time stomaching some of the off-the-cuff comments from the committee's liberals (one even worked into the conversation the line, "Some of my best friends are . . ."), but I felt that they served to balance the hostile looks and well-timed guffaws of the administrator.

After about two hours, the discussion began to wane. I remained keyed up, ready for anything, although the intensity of the discussion had drained me somewhat. "It's getting rather late," Doug Cabot said, glancing at his watch. "I'd like to start bringing this discussion to a close and allow Eric to get home before dawn. Are there any final questions?"

I glanced around the room. There were a few somber faces, a few smiles. Then the hospital administrator raised her voice again.

"I have one final question for Mr. Rofes," she said. "have you seen a psychiatrist about your problem?"

I was caught a little off guard. As I caught my breath and began to formulate a response, I noticed that many of the other trustees were obviously put off by her question.

"I don't believe I have a problem," I said. "I did see a psychiatrist while I was in college who helped me adjust to being gay, but currently I do not see one."

"Then my follow-up question is," she continued her hostile line of questioning. "Why are you doing this to us?"

Before I could answer, Doug Cabot jumped in. "I don't believe that this question merits a response from Eric. I apologize for —"

I cut him off. "Excuse me, Mr. Cabot," I said, "but I would

like a moment to respond to the question. I am not *doing* anything to you or to the school. I could have returned next year, written my gay articles under my own name, and have a major scandal come over the school without any preparation on the part of Miss Clarkson or the trustees. Or I could have walked away from education, robbing the school of another teacher simply because I didn't have the courage to discuss this difficult issue with all of you. I believe that I've chosen an honorable process by which to pursue the matter. I care about this school and I've tried to respond professionally and with sensitivity to everyone involved. I came here tonight prepared to answer questions as best as I could, however difficult and personal they might be. I also came here to be honest with you and not to cover up my political involvement or deceive you about my true thoughts on these matters.

"However, I did not come here to be insulted and I thank the rest of the trustees for their kindness and consideration this evening. It is one thing to find oneself in honest disagreement with others. It is quite another matter to find oneself insulted and I shall not accept any more of your questions."

With that off my chest, I sat there, red-faced, drained, angry and exhausted. I missed Doug Cabot's closing remarks as he summarized the evening's discussion and explained that I would now leave and the trustees would remain and discuss the issue. Since Alice was a part of the discussion, I would leave with Marie. I found myself shaking hands with my judges and being whisked by Marie out the door and into the cool night air.

Marie drove me home and came in to join me for a cup of coffee while I waited for the phone call from the school. Holly had a fresh pot of coffee ready for us when we walked in the door and she eagerly listened to Marie and me recount our tales of the inquisition.

"That hospital director sure sounds like the Anita Bryant of Shawmut Hills," Holly said. "I suppose there's going to be one in every crowd, but I'm glad you spoke your mind at the end."

"She was just terrible," Marie said shaking her head, "just terrible. I could tell that you were sitting there, trying to be polite, holding your feelings in and sitting on your temper. I don't know how you controlled yourself for as long as you did. You deserve some kind of medal for that performance, sweetie."

"So what are the odds that they'll keep you?" Holly asked. "I know it's hard to tell, especially since the phone might ring at any moment, but what's your prediction?"

I hesitated for a moment. "I think I made it crystal clear that this boy is going to be out — loud and proud — if he continues as a schoolteacher. The question will be whether they're willing to take the risk for the school. The way I see it, they need to weigh having a popular teacher who has somehow managed to earn a pretty decent reputation for academic competence against the fears that the conservative Shawmut Hills establishment might stop sending their kids to the school because a fag is on the faculty."

"What odds do you give me that they'll never find the chutzpah to keep you?" Holly asked. "I mean Shawmut Hills School just doesn't have a reputation for innovation and integrity."

"I don't know," Marie said slowly. "I think they might surprise us. I mean, I'm surprised that they're even considering the question, aren't you, Eric?"

"I guess deep inside me, I am. It really is a big step for the school to even allow the topic into the forum for discussion. And the fact that they're taking it seriously, considering the possiblities, is certainly a step, even if they decide against me."

"I'll bet they're just doing that because they're afraid you'll sue their asses off," Holly said, pouring coffee into our half-empty mugs.

"I'm not so sure of that," I responded quickly. "I give them more credit that that . . . but you might be right."

"It's difficult to call this one, Holly," Marie said. "Clearly there were some pretty cool characters at the meeting tonight who wouldn't care a bit about a homosexual teaching their kids. But there were some pretty hostile folks as well. In my mind, Cabot's going to be the swing vote. He's a pretty cagey guy and I don't think he showed his cards at all throughout the meeting."

Just then the telephone rang. I rushed to the front foyer and grabbed it before the third ring.

"Hello," I whispered into the receiver, clearly out of breath.

"Hello, is this Eric?"

"Yes it is. Who's calling please?" I asked in my most courteous tone of voice.

"This is Doug Cabot. We've just concluded our meeting and I've been asked to call you and let you know the decision of the committee."

His voice was calm, quiet, and I couldn't sense whether he was about to transmit good news or bad.

"We discussed the matter for about an hour. First of all, everyone was very appreciative of your willingness to answer our questions. We found the discussion to be quite informative. We thought that you conducted yourself in a mature and responsible manner throughout the evening."

He paused here. Get to the point, I thought, my mind racing madly.

"Thank you," I responded. "Did the committee reach a decision?"

"I'm getting to that," Cabot said slowly. "We would very much like to see you return to Shawmut Hills. Everyone feels that you're an excellent teacher and that we should do everything within our power to keep you here. We do feel, however, that — while it would be fine for you to be open about these things within our school community — we really couldn't allow you to use your real name in your writings, nor could we allow you to be photographed at gay events. We'd want you to keep your political activism low-key and away from controversy."

Again he paused, waiting for my reaction. I held my silence this time, forcing him to continue.

"You see, Eric, this school really couldn't stand the public attention that would come if word got out that we had a homosexual teacher. People would withdraw their children and our enrollment would fall. The entire financial stability of the school would be undermined. It's a risk that we could not take and still be a responsible board of trustees, even if we support you in principle.

"Thus we're hoping that you will return to the school next year, but without the same degree of activism."

I didn't know what to say. Yes, the school had made a major step by allowing me to return next year as a gay man, even if they were unwilling to allow me to be a public gay activist. On the other hand, the specific issues which I'd raised — leaving the pseudonyms behind, ending my enforced schizophrenia, feeling comfortable with media exposure — had been circumvented.

"It sounds as if you'd want me to come back, but on your own terms, not on mine," I said quietly.

"We prefer to think of it as, not in our terms or your terms, but in terms that have the best interests of the children in mind."

He was beginning to sound patronizing. "We don't want you to feel that you have to decide about this overnight. Take some time to think about it, maybe discuss it with your friends. But do let us know within the week."

I needed to clarify what he'd told me. This was all happening too quickly and my heart was pounding a mile a minute in my chest.

"If I return to Shawmut Hills," I asked, "what you're saying is that I still have to maintain two separate identities."

"You might choose to see it that way," Cabot acknowledged. "Your activist activities would have to be kept fully separate from your teaching."

"I'd still have to avoid photos and use a fake name?"

"I think you're correct in saying that," Cabot responded formally.

"Then what you're saying is that you don't want me to return next year, since I have made it very clear to you — both in my letter to Miss Clarkson and in the meeting this evening — that I intend to write under my own name next year."

"That's your decision, Eric."

"But it's *not* my decision. You're trying to absolve yourself and your board of trustees from this decision. You want me to be the one who decided not to return to the school. You don't even have the courage to tell me about your decision directly." I was beginning to shout.

"Now wait a minute, Eric. That's unfair —"

"No, you wait a minute, Mr. Cabot. I want you to answer me one question, and this time you listen carefully. I, Eric Rofes, am going to be an openly gay person next year, in my writing, in my political work, and in my teaching. Am I welcome to return to Shawmut Hills School next year, Mr. Cabot?"

There was a silence at the end of the line. I allowed him a moment to make the decision.

"Under those conditions, Eric, you would not be welcome back," he said slowly and quietly. Then he added, "But take a few days and think about it. We don't need your decision tonight."

"Thank you," I said. "I'm afraid I need to get off the phone now. I appreciate your call."

With that comment, I hung up the receiver, walked directly up the flight of stairs, went into my bedroom, and started to cry.

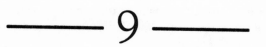

9

Once the final decision was made, I was determined to get through the final months of school as peacefully as possible. I put my anger and sadness aside and took on a public posture of support for the school and respect for the process that led to their decision to terminate my contract. I sent a gracious letter to Doug Cabot and the board, making clear my views on the situation and acknowledging their efforts to address the situation in what was usually a fairly humane and considerate manner. Wanting to make the best of my final weeks as a schoolteacher, and give my students my full energies, I sidestepped the many questions and comments that came my way.

Inside, I was burning up with anger. How could they do this to me? What right did they have to decide that I was unfit to work with children? This was my reward for my dedication, for the long hours I spent each weekend grading papers and preparing lessons? Who the hell did they think they were?

A tremendous sadness overcame me when I realized that I was leaving a career which I'd come to love. As long as it was important to me to be open about who I was — and to do the political work necessary to make sure this kind of thing was not allowed to happen to gay and lesbian teachers in the future — being a schoolteacher was not going to be an appropriate career choice. For all the enthusiasm I had for my work, my homosexuality made me unsuitable.

I knew that gay teachers in other parts of the country were starting to organize support groups. A notice I placed in local gay newspapers brought together several dozen homosexual teachers, administrators and school staff members. Only two of these people were openly gay and they taught in college programs. No one who taught children was able to be open about being gay. All of us, however, knew many faculty members in our schools who shared our sexual orientation.

One day, after the children had left on the school buses, I stopped by the library to see if Alice wanted to join me for a trip to the ice cream shop in Shawmut Center. I found her struggling to move a large movie projector from one side of the room to the other. After moving some of the obstacles out of her path, I sat down at her desk.

"Tell me, Eric," Alice said, wiping the dust from her clothing, "now that all the discussions are over, have you decided what you'll be doing for money next year? You seem filled with idealism and passion, but enthusiasm won't pay the rent. Even activists have to eat."

"There don't seem to be any schools around here that will hire an openly gay teacher," I told her.

"Did you make any of those calls I suggested?"

"Yes, last week I called the personnel departments of all the school systems you mentioned. I asked if they were hiring and, if so, if one's homosexuality would get in the way of being hired."

Alice looked interested. "And, what were the results of this survey?"

"The response was not very positive."

"I was afraid of that."

"What about private schools, Alice?" I asked. "Can you think of any private schools that can deal with this?"

"I don't know, my dear. I can't imagine a school like Shady Hill telling their parents that their lovely children in their Prep

Shop sweaters have a homosexual teacher. I think we're a few years away from that kind of liberalism in Massachusetts schools.

"The only school I can think of that would possibly be up for the challenge is a small, open-classroom school in Cambridge called the Fayerweather Street School. But they're so small that they only have six full-time teachers and there's tremendous competition for these positions on the rare occasions when they open up. I'd say you'd be wise to seek a new career."

The library door opened and Miss Clarkson walked in, noticed Alice and me chatting, gave her awkward greeting, then exited through another door.

"I just don't have the energy to deal with educating another principal, another school board, another faculty over these issues," I said to Alice. "I'm relieved that it's over, but I'm also exhausted, angry, and sad about the decision. I could probably use a few years' break from any kind of community education work."

Alice smiled up at me. "You should know what people are saying about you."

"What's that?"

"They're saying that you brought this all onto yourself by being so brazen about your personal life."

"Who's saying that?"

"Can't tell you that," Alice said, maintaining, as always, the confidentiality of her sources. "But I do have to tell you one other thing. I don't know of anyone at the school who doesn't respect you. Everyone is just amazed that you took on Clarkson and Cabot and the school board and that you're still functioning for the children. They're all in awe of you."

I had suspected that my trials had changed my stature among my peers, although the things that led me to feel this way were subtle, unspoken signals rather than overt comments. I knew that some teachers were angry and hostile toward me. One kindergarten teacher accused me of selfishness, refusing to sacrifice my own need to be open about my sex life for the sake of the children who needed me as their teacher. I tried to steel myself against the overt and subtle criticism, but I was counting down the days to the end of the school year and praying that I would manage to maintain my facade of equilibrium.

This became difficult to do when word leaked to the parents and students as to the reasons for my departure from the school. Doug Cabot was discussing my termination with a friend whose son was in my class during my initial year at Shawmut Hills while this man's wife was eavesdropping on an extension phone. The woman had not been particularly enamored of me during the time I worked with her child — primarily because I had refused to go along with her fantasy that her son was a brilliant and gifted student while he was, in fact, academically unimpressive. On hearing this gossip about me, she immediately went to her son and told him, "Mr. Rofes was fired because the school found out that he's a queer." Shawmut Hills' telephone wires went wild that evening as word passed from mother to mother about the circumstances surrounding my exit.

Several parents phoned me during the next day and asked me directly about these rumors. A hastily-organized meeting of parents saw Miss Clarkson informing them of the circumstances of the past several weeks, and allowed parents to ask questions and express their concerns. I was impressed with the depth of parent support for me and their overriding concern that their children have quality teachers — despite the teachers' sexual orientations. As one mother said at the meeting, "I want the best possible education for my son, and this school is making a big mistake by letting you go based on your personal life."

The meeting had the potential to develop into a mass movement to keep me at the school. A meeting with the children on the following day had similar potential. When I came upon a group of my students while on lunch duty one day and realized they were looking at me as if I had three heads, it was clearly time to talk.

The students had many questions about sexuality, gender roles, and all the issues related to adolescent sexual development. Their overwhelming concern, however, was with my future.

Would I be sent to jail? Did I worry about assassins? Would people be violent with me? I tried to calm their fears, explain the issues, and put to rest a difficult ordeal for all of us.

Because I was emotionally drained by my experience, I did not encourage a "Keep Mr. Rofes" movement. I actively discouraged such measures because I did not want this issue to rip the school apart and because I no longer had the personal commitment to continue at Shawmut Hills. While I believed that most people had dealt with a difficult and sensitive issue with courtesy and care, I felt that the process had finally succeeded in alienating me from the Shawmut Hills community. I did not belong here. Despite my positive feelings about my experiences with the children, I didn't have much in common with the values of this community. The suburban homes, dinner dances and church choirs had little to do with the day-to-day living of this leftist, Jewish, gay guy. I no longer belonged in a community to which I'd become attached. It was time to go home to Somerville.

One Saturday afternoon, during the final month of school, I was invited to lunch at a student's home in Shawmut Hills. On arriving at the house, I found it filled with my students and their parents, and decorated with streamers and colorful balloons. I'd walked into a "Farewell Mr. Rofes" party and I was overwhelmed with the kindness and support of my students and their families. Cards and presents were piled high on a table, a "thank you" cake sat displayed on a shelf, and I spent the afternoon finding a way to accept the appreciation and thanks of these parents. Parent after parent took me aside to express their thanks for the help and support I'd given their child during the year and wish me best of luck in my future work as a gay activist. While some parents were clearly more comfortable than others (one woman engaged me in a long conversation about homosexuality without ever saying the word), all of them were extending a hand to me which I gladly accepted.

On graduation day, I felt that eighteen students and one teacher were receiving their diplomas and being cast out into the

world. At the reception afterward in the schoolyard, Miss Clarkson pulled me aside for a few words.

"I want you to know, Eric," she said, "that I feel you've conducted yourself with a great deal of maturity these past few
months. On behalf of the school, I would like to thank you for
how well you've handled a difficult situation. I regret that the
problem could not be resolved in a way that was satisfactory for
everyone involved, but I do appreciate the way in which you've
dealt with the school, the parents and the children."

I thought for a moment and decided that now was as good a
time as any to make a request. "I hope that, should I ever return
to the teaching field, I'll be able to get a reference from you that
will be helpful to me in obtaining a position. Would you be open
to such a request from me?"

Miss Clarkson appeared a bit uncertain about how to respond
but said quickly, "Certainly, Eric, if I can be helpful to you, please
let me know."

"I want you to know just one thing," I said, trying to summon
up all the courage to make this final statement. "As much as I feel
you've been honorable in the way this whole thing proceeded, and
as much as I respect the honest struggle this school underwent to
try to understand the issues I've raised, I feel that you've made a
mistake and that this school has done something that is morally
without justification. I hope that someday I will be able to show
you that a school can hire an openly gay teacher, and have the
teacher and school succeed with parents and children alike. If I
ever find the opportunity again to be a teacher, I'm determined to
be as successful as possible to prove Shawmut Hills wrong."

Miss Clarkson looked me directly in the eye, extended her
hand, and said, "I do wish you the best of luck, Eric. Really, I do."

Epilogue
September, 1984

Leaving Shawmut Hills was painful and I avoided facing the intensity and confusion of my situation by throwing myself immediately into positions within Boston's gay community. I took a job as the features editor of *Gay Community News* which put me into a hotbed of controversy and debate on a daily basis. Our support group for gay teachers became the Boston Area Gay and Lesbian Schoolworkers and we spent the summer and fall of 1978 doing support work for activists in California who finally succeeded in defeating the anti-gay Briggs Initiative.

During August of that year, I received a call from Linda Brown, administrative assistant at the Fayerweather Street School in Cambridge. She'd heard that I'd left Shawmut Hills School and, since Fayerweather was looking for a teacher to head their middle school program, she decided to track me down and ask me to apply for the position.

My interview with the director of the school went well. At its conclusion, she explained that I was her favorite applicant for the position but that I'd have to go before a hiring committee of parents, board members and students in order to earn a contract at the school. She asked if I had any questions.

I decided it best to mention my special situation now, before proceeding further. I took a deep breath, looked her in the eye, and told her that I was gay and that I was an activist, and if this was going to cause problems, there'd be no need for me to go to any further interviews.

To my surprise the director responded to this news with a great deal of enthusiasm. She had several gay friends, was supportive of the gay liberation movement and, in fact, had recently hired an upfront lesbian to teach at Fayerweather. She didn't anticipate any problem with the hiring committee.

She was correct. I was awarded a contract to teach the middle school program at Fayerweather Street School and I spent the following five years teaching sixth, seventh and eighth graders in an open-classroom program. Contrary to the fears of the trustees at Shawmut Hills, class size expanded during my tenure at Fayerweather. When I arrived at the school, the middle school had seventeen students and there was much discussion among faculty members about discontinuing the program and limiting the school to kindergarten through fifth grade. I worked my hardest to develop a sound, creative academic program at the school and parents responded by sending their children to my classroom. When I left the school, forty-four children were enrolled in the middle school, forcing us to expand into larger quarters and to hire several additional teachers for the program.

While I wasn't always consciously aware of reacting off of the termination at Shawmut Hills, looking back at my five years at Fayerweather, I realize that I was driven with ambition in my desire to make the trustees at Shawmut Hills realize that their homophobia had cost the school one hell of a good teacher. I engaged my students in innovative projects, one of which resulted in the publication of our class project in book form. *The Kids' Book of Divorce* hit the stands in 1982 and brought my students and me a six-month publicity spin, including appearances on *The Today Show, 20/20, Evening Magazine,* and *Phil Donahue,* as well as feature articles in the *New York Times, Washington Post,* and *Newsweek.* Requests for copies poured in from around the world, we were interviewed by over a hundred media outlets, and the book was translated into Japanese the following year. Two additional books, *The Kids' Book About Parents* and *The Kids' Book About Death & Dying* have brought additional attention to the school and to my program.

Thus I became a high-profile schoolteacher while I continued my public gay activism. My lives coalesced and I stepped fully out of the closet. While televised interviews with me as an openly gay schoolteacher generally brought about a great deal of positive feedback (one piece was even nominated for a local Emmy award), I endured my share of hate mail, threatening phone calls, and hostile confrontations. Regardless of how nasty some people became, I was always aware that my position was immeasurably better than living a Dr. Jekyll and Mr. Hyde existence.

I haven't maintained contact with friends at Shawmut Hills School. Miss Clarkson left the school a year after my departure and many of my fellow teachers have gone on to other schools or other careers. Alice remains as the heart and soul of the school and it's through her that I keep tabs on my former students. A few incidents occurred this summer, however, which allowed me to finally put some of my feelings about my experience at Shawmut Hills at rest.

One evening, after seeing a movie, several friends and I stopped in at a local gay disco to dance. As I waited in line to check my coat, a tall, gangling guy came up to me and smiled.

"Hello, Mr. Rofes," he said. "Remember me?"

I had no idea who this person was in his rugby shirt, big blue eyes, and baseball cap. "No, I don't know who you are," I answered honestly. "How do you know me?"

And then my mind wandered back eight years, the gangly youth became an awkward sixth grader before my very eyes, and I realized I was seeing Jack — Stewart's "boyfriend" — before my eyes.

Now eighteen years old and attending a local college, Jack was in the process of coming out. He remembered my talk about homosexuality in my sex education class and thanked me "for the only bit of information that made me feel good about myself through my teenage years."

Jack told me that he'd thought about contacting me during high school, once he'd learned that I had left Shawmut Hills because I was gay, but he'd never had the courage. Still, he told me, the knowledge that a man he'd respected and liked was also homosexual, saved him a portion of the pain associated with coming out. He thanked me for my activism.

Several weeks later, on a local political television show, five people were debating the issue of gay rights. When a conservative gentleman raised his objections to homosexuals teaching in the schools, a woman named Doris Kearns rushed to defend gay teachers. She was a former assistant to President Johnson who had taught at Harvard, wrote an outstanding biography of LBJ, and is currently completing a book about the Kennedys; her son was one of my students in my second year at Shawmut Hills. "The best teacher my son ever had was a gay teacher," she said on live television. "In fact, right now he's the president of one of Boston's largest gay political groups. I'd fight for the rights of gay people to teach school any day."

And finally, what became of the board of trustees which voted to let me go? Most of the trustees I never heard from again. One trustee who teaches anthropology at a local school, began inviting me to discuss homosexuality with her high school students five years ago and I've returned each year to be "gay person on display." Another invited me over to dinner during the following year, confessed that her brother was gay, and apologized for being unable to support me more strongly.

The biggest surprise, however, came last month as I wandered through the Labor Day crowd during tea dance at the Boatslip, the famed outdoor party area for gay men in Provincetown. A short man with dark glasses came up to me and said, "Eric Rofes! Remember me?"

I had no idea who this man was.

"It's me, Andrew Singer. Remember, I was a parent at Shawmut Hills School and I was a trustee at the time we voted to terminate your contract."

It was the psychiatrist from Massachusetts General; I'd heard he was not very helpful to me during the debate over whether to remove me from the school.

"Oh, yes," I said quietly. "I remember you."

"Boy, I was in a tough position sitting on that committee. I was just coming out at the time. There wasn't much that one person could have done to help you keep your job. It was a losing battle from the start."

I stared at this man and felt a mixture of fury and pity. How could this closet case stab me in the back? How could he live with himself today? Isn't it always those who are wrestling with homosexual feelings themselves who are the biggest enemies of gay rights?

"Of course, I'm divorced now myself and I've found a nice place to live in Boston. I like my lifestyle and I've followed your career in the newspapers. Let me just say how glad I am that you were able to find a teaching position that was 'comfortable' for you. Shawmut Hills was no place for you. I'm glad to see you've done well."

I looked this man over from head to toe and I didn't know what to say. I smiled at him. "Nice seeing you, Mr. Singer. Nice seeing you." And I turned and continued my walk through the holiday crowd.

Other books of interest from Alyson Publications

☐ **ONE TEENAGER IN TEN: Writings by gay and lesbian youth,** edited by Ann Heron, $4.00. One teenager in ten is gay; here, twenty-six young people tell their stories: of coming to terms with being different, of the decision how — and whether — to tell friends and parents, and what the consequences were.

☐ **THE PEARL BASTARD,** by Lillian Halegua, $4.00. Frankie is fifteen when she leaves her large, suffocating Catholic family. Here, with painful innocence and acute vision, she tells the story of her sudden entry into a harsh maturity, beginning with the man in the fine green car who does not mourn the violent death of a seagull against his windshield.

☐ **THE TWO OF US,** by Larry Uhrig, $7.00. The author draws on his years of counseling with gay people to give some down-to-earth advice about what makes a relationship work. He gives special emphasis to the religious aspects of gay unions.

☐ **THE LAVENDER COUCH,** by Marny Hall, $8.00. Here is a guide to the questions that should be considered by lesbians or gay men considering therapy or who are already in it: How do you choose a good therapist? What kind of therapy is right for you? When is it time to leave therapy?

☐ **BETWEEN FRIENDS,** by Gillian E. Hanscombe, $7.00. Frances and Meg were friends in school years ago; now Frances is a married housewife while Meg is a lesbian involved in progressive politics. Through letters written between these women and their friends, the author weaves an engrossing story while exploring many vital lesbian and feminist issues.

☐ **IN SUCH DARK PLACES,** by Joseph Caldwell, $7.00. This impressive novel about a not-so-liberated gay man's conflict with love and faith, isolation and commitment, was praised by *Saturday Review* for its "vivid portraits and unforgettable scenes." By Joseph Caldwell, winner of the Rome Prize.

☐ **QUATREFOIL,** by James Barr, $7.00. Originally published in 1950, this book marks a milestone in gay writing: it introduced two of the first non-stereotyped gay characters to appear in American fiction. This story of two naval officers who become lovers gave readers of the fifties a rare chance to counteract the negative imagery that surrounded them.

☐ **REFLECTIONS OF A ROCK LOBSTER: A story about growing up gay,** by Aaron Fricke, $5.00. When Aaron Fricke took a male date to the senior prom, no one was surprised: he'd gone to court to be able to do so, and the case had made national news. Here Aaron tells his story, and shows what gay pride can mean in a small New England town.

☐ **YOUNG, GAY AND PROUD,** edited by Sasha Alyson, $4.00. Here is the first book ever to address the needs and problems of a mostly invisible minority: gay youth. Questions about coming out to parents and friends, about gay sexuality and health care, about finding support groups, are all answered here; and several young people tell their own stories.

☐ **COMING OUT RIGHT, A handbook for the gay male,** by Wes Muchmore and William Hanson, $6.00. The first steps into the gay world — whether it's a first relationship, a first trip to a gay bar, or coming out at work — can be full of unknowns. This book will make it easier. Here is advice on all aspects of gay life for both the inexperienced and the experienced.

☐ **LIFETIME GUARANTEE,** by Alice Bloch, $7.00. Here is the personal and powerfully-written chronicle of a woman faced with the impending death of her sister from cancer, at the same time that she must also face her family's reaction to her as a lesbian.

☐ **ALL-AMERICAN BOYS,** by Frank Mosca, $5.00. "I've known that I was gay since I was thirteen. Does that surprise you? It didn't me. . . ." So begins *All-American Boys,* the story of a teenage love affair that should have been simple — but wasn't.

☐ **THE MOVIE LOVER,** by Richard Friedel, $7.00. The entertaining coming-out story of Burton Raider, who is so elegant that as a child he reads *Vogue* in his playpen. "The writing is fresh and crisp, the humor often hilarious," writes the *L.A. Times.*

☐ **DECENT PASSIONS,** by Michael Denneny, $7.00. What does it mean to be in love? Do the joys outweigh the pains? Those are some of the questions explored here as Denneny talks separately with each member of three unconventional relationships — a gay male couple, a lesbian couple, and an interracial couple — about all the little things that make up a relationship.

☐ **DANCER DAWKINS AND THE CALIFORNIA KID,** by Willyce Kim, $6.00. Dancer Dawkins views life best from behind a pile of hotcakes. Her lover, Jessica Riggins, has fallen into the clutches of Fatin Satin Aspen. Meanwhile, Little Willie Gutherie of Bangor, Maine, renames herself The California Kid, stocks up on Rubbles Dubble bubble gum, and heads west. When this crew collides in San Francisco, what can be expected? Just about anything. . . .

☐ **LEGENDE,** by Jeannine Allard, $6.00. Sometime in the last century, two women living on the coast of France, in Brittany, loved each other. They had no other models for such a thing, so one of them posed as a man for most of their life together. This legend is still told in Brittany; from it, Jeannine Allard has created a hauntingly beautiful story of two women in love.

I would welcome feedback and comments on this book. They may be sent to me at:
Eric Rofes
Box 1430
Back Bay Annex
Boston, Mass. 02117